THE ONE QUEST

A MAP OF THE WAYS OF TRANSFORMATION

Books by Claudio Naranjo

Character and Neurosis: An Integrative View

The Divine Child and the Hero:
Inner Meaning in Children's Literature

The End of Patriarchy
and the Dawning of a Tri-une Society

Ennea-type Structures:
Self-Analysis for the Seeker

The Enneagram of Society:
Healing the Soul to Heal the World

Enneatypes in Psychotherapy

Gestalt Therapy: The Attitude and Practice
of an Atheoretical Experientialism

The Healing Journey

How to Be

The One Quest

The Psychology of Meditation

Techniques of Gestalt Therapy

Transformation Through Insight:
Enneatypes in Life,
Literature and Clinical Practice

The Way of Silence
and the Talking Cure

THE ONE QUEST

A Map of the Ways of Transformation

CLAUDIO NARANJO

Since we have learned the Alphabet of Love,
None other text than this one we repeat:
With the heart's eyes, wide-opened now, behold
Whate'er thou seest as but a form of His!

—SAADI

A Gateways Consciousness Classic

Gateways Books and Tapes
Nevada City, California

Published by Gateways Books and Tapes
P.O. Box 370
Nevada City, CA 95959
800.869.0658 or 530.477.8101
www.gatewaysbooksandtapes.com

First published in 1972 by The Viking Press, Inc.
New York City, New York
Library of Congress catalog card number: 79-158418
Earlier ISBN: 0670-52639-8
Ballantine Books edition, 1973 ISBN: 0-3452356-9-X

ISBN: 978-0-89556-161-1

Library of Congress Cataloging-in-Publication Data

Naranjo, Claudio.
  The one quest : a map of the ways of transformation /
Claudio
  Naranjo.
      p. cm.
  Originally published: New York : Viking Press, 1972.
  Includes bibliographical references and index.
  ISBN 0-89556-161-1 (978-89556-161-9 : alk. paper)
  1. Self-realization. I. Title.
  BJ1470.N37 2006
  158.1--dc22
          2005035915

ACKNOWLEDGMENTS

Delacorte Press and George Allen & Unwin Ltd.: From *The Master Game: Pathways to Higher Consciousness beyond the Drug Experience* by Robert S. deRopp. Copyright © 1968 by Robert S. deRopp. A Seymour Lawrence Book/Delacorte Press. Reprinted by permission of the publisher.

E. P. Dutton & Co., Inc., and Jonathan Cape Ltd.: From the book *Tales of the Dervishes* by Idries Shah. Copyright © 1967 by Idries Shah. Reprinted by permission of the publishers.

Harper & Row, Publishers, Inc., and Chatto and Windus Ltd.: From *The Doors of Perception* by Aldous Huxley. Copyright 1954 by Aldous Huxley. Reprinted by permission of the publishers.

Humanities Press, Inc., New York, and George Allen & Unwin Ltd.: From *Integral Yoga* by Haridas Chaudhari.

Hutchinson & Company: From *The Way of the White Clouds: A Buddhist Pilgrim in Tibet* by Anagarika B. Govinda.

The New American Library, Inc.: From Dante, *The Divine Comedy*, "Purgatorio," translated by John Ciardi. Copyright © 1957, 1959, 1960, 1961 by John Ciardi.

Oxford University Press: From *Tibetan Book of the Dead*, edited by W. Y. Evans-Wentz.

Psychology Today: From "The Psychology of the Samurai" by Robert Frager. Reprinted from *Psychology Today* magazine, January 1969. Copyright © Communications/Research/Machines, Inc.

Princeton University Press and Routledge and Kegan Paul Ltd.: From *The Collected Works of C. G. Jung*, ed. by G. Adler, M. Fordham, and H. Read, trans. by R. F. C. Hull, Bollingen Series XX, vol. 11, *Psychology and Religion: West and East*, "Psychological Commentary on 'The Tibetan Book of the Dead,'" (Copyright © 1958 and 1969 by Bollingen Foundation). Reprinted by permission.

Real People Press: From *Person to Person: The Problem of Being Human*, by Carl Rogers and Barry Stevens. © Real People Press, 1967.

Van Nostrand Reinhold Company: From *Toward a Psychology of Being* by Abraham H. Maslow. © 1968 by Litton Educational Publishing, Inc. Reprinted by permission of Van Nostrand Reinhold Company.

In the opinion of the Editors, this text as it stands is still the best non-partisan overview of the approaches to human development, in its broader and most fundamental sense, which has been produced within an academic environment in order to clarify thinking on educational policy.

—*Encyclopedia of World Problems and Human Potential*
(K.G. Saur) referencing the research report
The Unfolding of Man (later published as *The One Quest*)

TABLE OF CONTENTS

IV THE ONENESS OF EXPERIENCE IN HE WAYS OF GROWTH   123

FOREWORD

The re-issue of Claudio Naranjo's *The One Quest*, a classic in the literature on consciousness, provides us with an opportunity to reflect on the career of a remarkable man who has left an unmistakable, complex imprint on the exploration of consciousness and human development. Naranjo has made significant contributions in such diverse areas as research on psycho-active drugs (pioneering, for instance, the study of MDMA and Ayahuasca), on Gestalt therapy, on what is now the Hoffman Quadrinity method, on meditation, including the "dynamic meditation" later espoused by Osho (Rajneesh), and a variety of other approaches including, most recently, the Enneagram.

As this volume shows, there is a unity in this complex diversity. That unity is "the one quest" for human growth, development, and self-realization. In this masterful volume, Naranjo presents the One Quest as a project that crosses Education, Psychotherapy, Religion, and includes Ways of Action, Feeling, Knowledge, and Mindfulness. This book was originally commissioned by Stanford Research Institute, and in its first form, entitled "The Unfolding of Man," it was incorporated into an *International Encyclopedia of Human Problems and Resources*. Idries Shah refers to *The One Quest* (in that original format) in a footnote in his book *The Dermis Probe* in this complimentary way:

Few people are as yet aware how traditional materials of this kind [teaching stories] are receiving the attention of scientific researchers. An interesting recent example is a research memorandum "The Unfolding of Man" by the distinguished professor Claudio Naranjo carried out through the Stanford Research Institute and supported by the U.S. Office of Education, Bureau of Research, Washington. Only a few years ago any investigation of human transformation under such distinguished auspices would have been unthinkable.

—The Dermis Probe
(latest edition 1980, Octagon Press)

In the Introduction, Naranjo writes,

As well as being a book on psychotherapeutic and religious issues, this is a book about education—yet I say little about education in particular. This is because I regard everything as a statement about education. Education is not only "one more" domain of culture, but a microcosm of them all. Education is culture being passed on—and is inseparable from culture's very nature. Education only becomes an independent field of endeavor to the extent that it becomes the art of science of deliberate transmission of cultural attainments. Even in this sense, the whole of this book is about education: its subject matter is the intentional transmission of culture, in the essential meaning of the word.

Naranjo goes on to explain that,

Culture is a matter of culturing or cultivation, and that it has the same origin as the word agriculture. Culture is not something that we can have, but something that we are: We are cultivated to the extent that we have grown up. Similarly, to cultivate is to grow people.

This thoughtful and original frame is presented in the typically elegant and understated way that Naranjo expresses himself throughout this book. In a few sentences, Naranjo weaves culture and education, two misunderstood and often maligned words, into a much broader and richer framework of meaning. Rather than being obstacles to self-realization, Naranjo reframes them as central dimensions, indeed as constitutive, of human self-realization, and used them as a focal point to articulate self-realization in a way that does justice to the complexities of human experience.

And yet Naranjo's depth of insight might get lost precisely because he doesn't hit us over the head with this frame, he doesn't try to "sell it" or present it with great fanfare. This is a book that bears careful reading, because virtually every page is littered with such insights and fresh perspectives. For instance, in the brief discussion of Jung and Gestalt, Naranjo seems to distill the essence of these complex and rich approaches into a few beautifully written pages, illuminating them anew for the scholar, and providing an inviting angle of approach for the novice.

Naranjo's own quest has continued along the path developed in this book. Most recently we have seen the publication of the important volume on *The Enneagram of Society,* and a much anticipated volume on education is forthcoming. They can be seen as a broader effort to address the culture of cultivation and the cultivation of culture, a way to reflect on the interrelationship between individual and society, and an approach that does not see growth as "the acquisition of traits or attributes borrowed from without," a mere collection of tools.

Naranjo was clearly a pioneer in many different aspects of human growth, but I believe this present volume can also be seen as an original contribution—and indeed a path-breaking one—to a field that did not exist when this book was written. I am speaking of Transformative Education. Naranjo's broad umbrella of Psychotherapy, Religion, and Education is an integration at the leading edge of the recent efforts to develop transformative education. This volume, besides being a classic of the literature on consciousness and human development that deserves to be read simply for that reason, also offers a wonderful introduction to the wide range of possibilities and perspectives that can inform transformative learning and transformative education today.

The One Quest is a remarkable integration of many perspectives on human development, on culture and education, written by a man who has the comprehensive intelligence to bring all the different strands together. Through the depth of insight in these pages, we can see Naranjo's education is not just a possession, but a quality of his being.

Alfonso Montuori, Ph.D.
California Institute of Integral Studies, September 2005

AUTHOR'S PREFACE TO THE 2005 EDITION

At the time this book was written its point of view was controversial, and now it has become commonplace. I refer to the view of a convergence of the many spiritual, therapeutic and educational paths upon a common goal—a single end-state of human development. The value of the book lies not so much in its inspiring idea or vision, however, but in the way that this vision is presented, and I trust that the analysis I have undertaken of psycho-spiritual technologies and of the nature of transformation will be of interest today as it was in the late sixties.

When I wrote most of this book (in 1968) comparative religion was well established but the comparative consideration of the therapeutic and spiritual domains had not gone beyond Allan Watts' Psychotherapy East and West. Nobody had attempted yet the comparative study of psycho-spiritual methodologies—which is my present subject.

Those who read these pages over thirty years after they were written may miss in them the reference to therapeutic schools of spiritual movements that have become prominent since then; but I hope it is clear that to regard this a book about specific paths would miss its point—which is showing how different techniques or procedures relate to each other and how they constitute embodiment of deeper issues. More than a book about this or that, it is one about how things hang together, and the synthesis that it spells out proved fruitful in my own work as a creator and director of a psycho-spiritual school that continues to evolve.

I hope that it may be of inspiration to seekers and also to those who occupy themselves in assisting others along the path.

—Claudio Naranjo

AN INTRODUCTION TO
THE QUEST FOR GROWTH

The Contemporary Scene

Men have felt throughout the centuries that their generation was a period of evolution more significant than the preceding ones. History has been rich in change since the dawn of
civilization, and the perceptive individuals of each epoch have
noted the particular nature of the evolution (or decadence) oc-
curring in their own time and place. A common error in perspective often led them to believe that what was closest to
them was the most important crisis in centuries, or even the
prelude to the millennium. Although it may be an error in
perspective on my part too, I share the impression of many
that our time is one of drastic transformation, a time of very
profound crisis: the death of one culture and the sprouting of
another.

We are questioning and taking leave from cultural forms,
institutions, and sources of authority. I emphasize questioning

and taking leave rather than rebelling because, just as in the physical world a revolution is a circular movement that ends where it started, again and again in historical revolutions the son supplants the father only to grow up in his likeness. Those whom I see as the flesh of today's "revolution" are not rebelling so much as they are questioning, departing, leaving something behind, and "minding their own business." This seems to be much more drastic than the emotional reaction of protest. For it is clear that when we leave something behind we are seeking a fresh start or we have already developed something that renders obsolete what we are leaving. One might even say that today the broad cultural divisions of religion, art, reason, standards of morality, and political institutions are "dead"; at least this is how they are now being experienced by a growing number of people. They are left behind, as a snake leaves behind its old skin, unchanged and still beautiful perhaps, but too tight, and therefore not functional.

This abandonment of forms has left not only an emptiness but a thirst, not only meaninglessness but a search for meaning. Mechanical repetition has rendered the old formulas trite, and a groping for orientation has arisen. As "solutions" become questionable, we awaken to the problems. As we lose faith in our ideals and hopes, we experience despair; as we see our dreams as mere dreams and our assumptions as mere assumptions, we are brought face to face with a sense of limitation, incompleteness, and deference to the unknown.

That a problem may be of greater value than a solution, a question than an answer, a longing than a contentment, are thoughts that have been voiced many times before. Socrates said, "I only know what I know not." For Kierkegaard despair—the "sickness unto death"—was inseparable from the authentic life. Krishnamurti, weary of the limitations imposed by beliefs, dogmas, and even "methods," significantly entitled one of his books *Freedom from the Known.*[1] *

It is not difficult to conceive that questioning may be more creative than an attachment to ready-made answers. Iconoclasm rejects symbols and seeks the source of meaning beyond the outward form. If a measure of iconoclasm can be healthy even in the face of valid "solutions," how much more so in the face of pseudosolutions to which we cling in order to preserve our peaceful sleep? After all, it is from a questioning, seeking, and even desperate state of mind that all the values that we cherish originally emerged. The water that quenched the thirst of our forefathers may not be the water we need today; it must be found afresh each time and cannot be stored.

I suppose that most of us have experienced cycles of achievement, the realization of certain goals, or episodes of withdrawal from action when we paused to reflect upon our direction and the meaning of our purpose. Goal-seeking alternates with goal-setting, as planning does with building. Can we say that one is of greater importance than the other? Our culture is like a tree that sheds its leaves in autumn. The leaves were beautiful and useful. Others will take their place in the spring, and will serve their function too. The source of this renewal is the tree's need. To paste dead leaves on the twigs is to create a false fulfillment. The value of a tree in winter is not in its leaves or in its blossoms, but in its function as a silent laboratory; its withdrawal into itself. Our silent evolution today is also one of withdrawal or inwardness in which we forsake our visible cares in order to turn to those of our roots. From the form we turn to the formlessness of that which seeks to be born or expressed; from instrumentality we turn to the need from which instruments derive their meaning. But what is it that

* Numbered reference notes begin on page 231.

takes place in that inwardness into which we retire? It can be formulated as a concern with issues of personal growth, self-perfecting, or personality change. It is this longing, expressed through ventures variously understood as "psychotherapy," "mysticism," or "experimental education" that is the realm of this book.

The departure from familiar forms and solutions has generally led to two different, though compatible, reactions. One is an openness to unfamiliar answers provided by cultures other than our own—Zen, Buddhism, Taoism, Vedanta, Sufism, esotericism, and even shamanism. The other is more experimental and seeks the development of fresh possibilities—encounter groups, dianetics, sensory deprivation, new mind-changing chemicals, and so on.

The interest in ancient views of the human predicament can be seen in the increased output of literature and in the emergence of bookstores that specialize in this area. Many of the Oriental classics are being translated into English and no longer constitute reading matter for Orientalists alone. Would we have anticipated twenty years ago that a work like *The Tibetan Book of the Dead* would appear in a paperback edition or that the *I Ching* would become a best seller in the United States? There are also recent works by such Eastern authors as Daisetz T. Suzuki, Idries Shah, and Swami Nikhilananda, as well as other volumes by Westerners who have been deeply steeped in foreign traditions: Lama Govinda, Mircea Eliade, Karlfried von Durkheim, Alan Watts, Heinrich Zimmer, Christmas Humphreys, and Piotr Ouspenski, to name just a few. The traditions with which these authors deal emphasize the need for a "personal transmission," oral communication, and, in particular, guidance in a practical discipline. However, the need that finds some satisfaction in reading is not intellectual. It is a need which seeks a nourishment words can only hint at. No wonder, then, that along with the increased demand for books of this type we find an increased demand for spiritual teachers or gurus. But with persons as with books an intensive need is not always discriminating and will cling to anything that has the appearance of being relevant. Unquestionably the longing of the new generation has brought onto the scene (or the market) a number of self-styled teachers, American and Asian, who either profit monetarily or derive personal satisfaction from playing the "master" game, and cultish groups increase their self-esteem by soliciting converts. Yet these are peripheral and pathological manifestations of a valid need, and the activity of earnest persons and groups should not be judged on the basis of these fringe elements as most of the great Eastern traditions presently have authoritative channels in the West.

The exploratory or experimental answer to our contemporary longing is most clearly represented by the burst of activity that one sees in the field of psychotherapy. A consequence of this activity is a breaking down of old boundaries and a new perspective or professional intent. This proliferation of novel concepts and techniques has been the object of at least two synthetic formulations, one theoretical and the other practical. At the theoretical level it was Abraham H. Maslow who first drew attention to the unity of orientation that underlies many of the developments of present-day psychology. It was he who introduced the notion of the Third Psychology, or the Third Force in psychology, expressions that have now become standard. His own words in the preface of *Toward a Psychology of Being* are at this point more appropriate than my own:

> The two comprehensive theories of human nature most influencing psychology until recently have been the Freudian and the experimental-positivistic-behavioristic. All other theories were less

comprehensive and their adherents formed many splinter groups. In the last few years, however, these various groups have rapidly been coalescing into a third, increasingly comprehensive theory of human nature, into what might be called a "Third Force." This group includes the Adlerians, Rankians, and Jungians, as well as all the neo-Freudians (or neo-Adlerians) and the post-Freudians (psychoanalytic ego-psychologists as well as writers like Marcuse, Wheelis, Marmor, Szasz, N. Brown, H. Lynd, and Schachtel, who are taking over from the Talmudic psychoanalysts). In addition, the influence of Kurt Goldstein and his organismic-psychology is steadily growing. So also is that of Gestalt therapy, of the Gestalt and Lewinian psychologists, of the general-semanticists, and of such personality-psychologists as G. Allport, G. Murphy, J. Moreno and H. A. Murray. A new and powerful influence is existential psychology and psychiatry. Dozens of other major contributors can be grouped as Self-psychologists, phenomenological psychologists, growth-psychologists, Rogerian psychologists, humanistic psychologists, and so on and so on and so on. A full list is impossible.[2] *

On a practical level the rough equivalent to the Third Psychology is best represented by a new institution: the "growth center." A special term, the Eupsychian Network, was introduced by Maslow to designate those informally related institutes which, because of their overlapping goals, can be considered a part of this group. Most growth centers are places where the allied interests of many diverse techniques, gener-

* Maslow also suggests the following: "A simpler way of grouping these is available in the five journals in which this group is most apt to publish, all relatively new. These are the *Journal of Individual Psychology* (University of Vermont, Burlington, Vt. 05401), the *American Journal of Psychoanalysis* (220 West 98th Street, New York, N.Y. 10025), the *Journal of Existential Psychiatry* (679 North Michigan Avenue, Chicago, Ill. 60611), the *Review of Existential Psychology and Psychiatry* (Duquesne University, Pittsburgh, Penn. 15219) and the newest one, the *Journal of Humanistic Psychology* (2637 Marshall Drive, Palo Alto, Calif. 94303). In addition, the journal *Manas* (P.O. Box 32, 112 El Sereno Station, Los Angeles, Calif. 90032) applies this point of view to the personal and social philosophy of the intelligent layman."[3]

ally derived from psychotherapy and the arts, are implicitly acknowledged and made available to the community in the form of intensive programs. However, the function of these institutions has gone beyond the therapeutic service that people have sought in the office of the specialist. At least three aspects of current developments can allow us to appreciate their impact:

(1) We might say that the growth centers provide "tasting programs" that minimize the chances of the individual espousing a *way* before experiencing premarital dating. The very existence of the center and the nature of the activities which are carried out there can affect the people of the community. They can become aware of the issue of human development, of the varied means available to satisfy the existing need, and of the convergence or complementarity of different methods which goes beyond the restrictive formulations of individual groups. This last realization has been instrumental in counteracting the tendency of the individual to become attached, and addicted, to a specific idea, technique, or cult, thus missing the occasion to explore different ways and finding the experience which is for him the most fruitful.

(2) By providing an opportunity for professional intercommunication, some of the growth centers have had a significant, though informal and subtle, impact upon the development of present-day psychological techniques. Prominent individuals who formerly worked in isolation may now be in residence at a single location and thus have access to one another's ideas, which may complement or enrich their own. This cannot happen through the medium of the written word for so much in therapeutic practice is nonverbal and undescribed and cannot be conceptualized without loss of its essence. This growth of specific approaches into more encompassing systems is now taking place continually in a way that is not reflected in publi-

cations. Encounter-group techniques have assimilated much from sensory awareness, psychosynthesis, and Gestalt therapy; Gestalt therapy has assimilated concepts from sensory awareness, psychodrama, and encounter; psychosynthesis, from Gestalt therapy and autogenic training; psychodrama, from encounter and bioenergetics—and so on. It is an interchange which becomes unavoidable because of the eclectic programs sponsored by the centers.

(3) Esalen Institute can be regarded as the beginning of the explicit concern with the affective domain in education and the "human-potentialities movement." Created by Michael Murphy and Richard Price, Esalen offered its first residential program in 1966. It was the first institute of its type and served as a model for many others. Although it continues to offer numerous brief programs to the community at large, during recent years one of Esalen's objectives has been the operation of a college for selected individuals who may be able to use "experimental-learning" techniques in their fields of activity. Its residential program realized Murphy's dream of making Aldous Huxley's conception of education an actuality: a learning experience designed to teach what Huxley called the "nonverb of humanities." Man is an amphibian, Huxley said, living in many worlds at the same time: a world of reason, a world of perception, a world of movement, a world of visceral activity, a world of possible mystical experiences, and several others. But for centuries the education we have received has simply stressed the development of reason and transmission of information, and now many of our other faculties lie dormant or function in aberrant ways. Huxley pinpointed a number of techniques, old and new, which were developed in order to educate the senses, feelings, the system of action, and so on, and he suggested that they be incorporated into the educational system. Murphy decided that this goal could be more immedi-

ately achieved through a program which encompassed those aspects of education that schools leave out. Other programs then followed in similar growth centers and fragments of the original were soon adapted for use by some schools.

Contemporary life must take into account the creative bubbling of the new approaches to human development just described, and it must also take into account the growing openness to the traditions of previous decades and centuries which in our prejudiced arrogance we have ignored. Even if God is "dead" in the Western church, he is still alive in the experience of individuals who do not invoke his name. A modern theologian has remarked:

> The sanctuary is so seldom filled with vitality and enthusiasm. The words are still there: "celebration," "joy," "hope," and "love." But the music drags and there is no dancing and little radical openness to surprise and change. In my experience, the substance of wonder is more frequently found in the prose of the secular than in the often quaint poetry of religion. The sacred is in the profane; the holy in the quotidian; the wonder is the world.[4]

But although formal religion may be dead, the source of its forms is closer than ever to man. Today's religion is a religion of peak-experiences or, to borrow a phrase from the psychedelic culture, it is a religion of "turning on."

Employing a more restricted definition than other specialists, Professor Gershom G. Scholem equates mysticism with the romantic stage of religious development rather than with its experimenting source. To him, religions originate in a consciousness of unity, in which the division between man and the divine has not taken place, and where the presence of God does not need to be experienced in an exceptional state of rapture. This is followed by institutional religion, the "classical stage" in religious development, which sets a gulf between

God, the transcendental Being, and finite creatures. This is the condition for the emergence of mysticism. Mysticism "strives to piece together the fragments broken by the religious cataclysm, to bring back the old unity which religion has destroyed, but on a new plane, where the world of mythology and that of revelation meet in the soul of man." [5]

If we accept Scholem's interpretation of the term, we can say that the present is the dawn of a mystical era. Yet, there is a difference between this second mystical era and that which extended from the twelfth to the sixteenth century: whereas past mystics expressed their experiences in terms of their tradition, those of today disregard the language and symbols of the Christian heritage and prefer either created or imported images and nomenclature. For this reason it can be maintained that despite the search and even the achievements that generally pertain to the domain of mysticism "religion is dead." The traditions to which people are turning have been classed by historians as "religious" only for want of a better term and because of the lack of an appropriate concept in our culture. Zen Buddhists, for instance, again and again assert that Zen is not a religion, but "a special mode of transmission outside of the scriptures." "The *Vedanta*," René Guénon explains, "contrary to an opinion widely held among orientalists, is neither a philosophy nor a religion. . . . Deliberately to consider this doctrine under these aspects is one of the gravest errors, calculated to result in failure to understand anything about it from the outset; . . . religion . . . is something wholly Western . . ." [6] It is with this trans-religious domain, or whatever name we give to it, that today's man is increasingly concerned. Religion is in autumnal foliage. The domain we discuss is within the roots, or within the ripening seed, in which the tree both ends and begins.

What mysticism is to religion, encounter is to personal relationships. I am not speaking here of encounter groups specifically, though these, like Gestalt groups, T-groups, and others, are occasions for the coming face to face of persons who are attempting to communicate with authenticity, forgetting social rules, roles, and games. The encounter process is necessarily destructive of forms, for it is unstructured by definition and may be, when properly guided, an explosive experience which leads to moments of revelation and even rapture. "One of the goals of education should be to teach that Life is precious," writes Maslow. "If there were no joy in Life, it would not be worth living." Human relationships today are like an expanse of deadness with patches of intense life where this preciousness is being discovered. And just as mysticism is a technique of solitary ecstasy that permits one to overcome a state of inner (and cultural) schism, we now have techniques of social ecstasy that make the restitution of contact between basically estranged individuals possible. It is a means for those who are alienated, but longing and ready to give up their total isolation.

Encounter is by no means limited to the remedial or educational situation. To an increasing extent people are learning to be themselves in other aspects of their lives. The notion of right and wrong derived from anonymous authority is giving way to the idea that "everything goes if the parties agree," and thus people are exploring their inborn sense of preference or rightness. Normative goodness is dying, but intrinsic goodness cannot die. People are rediscovering the preciousness of life that was veiled rather than revealed by existing statements. We hear that human relationships are schizoid (Rollo May), mercantile (Erich Fromm), and alienated (Karen Horney), but in the midst of this deadness we can see the emergence of new life. The time will probably come when a completely new foliage of social forms will evolve. Man, in an unacknowledged thirst for self-knowledge, once set out to explore the whole universe. Disappointed but hopeful he now turns with his amassed knowledge toward himself. Today the value is in the search, in the exploration of chaos and of identities, in the renewal of meanings. This expression of yearning in the midst of a dying speculative philosophy is a return to the Problem of Man and a bowing of reason to experience, both dominant traits of existentialism which, among present philosophies, seems to monopolize all vitality. But just as philosophy in turning to Man generated existentialism, science, in turning to Man, generated today's psychology and sociology. Yet, even within the dawn of psychology there has been a conceptual transition from the mechanics of behavior—man the robot—to the properly human aspects of man the pilot. For the first time, physiologists and psychologists have begun to speak of a "science of consciousness."

Toward a Science of Growth

Other countries, for example India and Tibet, have had diversified spiritual technologies. Now that geographical boundaries and distances mean little, we are incorporating the sum of these diversities and adding it to our own. The result is not the organized variety of an English garden, but the chaotic abundance of a marketplace. The need for personal development, self-realization, orientation, identity, or whatever we choose to name contemporary longing, coupled with today's rapid technology, has resulted in access to a variety of psychotherapeutic, educational, or mystical methods never known before.

In speaking of the Third Psychology, Maslow perceived certain family resemblances between some of the modern ways of dealing with the psyche. A recent book, edited by Herbert Otto and John Mann, which contains information about some of the newer means, bears the suggestive title *Ways of Growth*,[7] an expression that I will frequently use.* However, putting these ways into a single taxonomical drawer is still far from putting an end to chaos. More often than not, the representatives of each system continue to say "I have the truth." Also, the Third Psychology is only one family among others: the Freudian, the behavioristic, and the imports from the East or from the past. Are we to believe that the truth is only in one of the many approaches, the others being only approximations? Or is the historical fact that they are all in demand an indication that there is a measure of effectiveness in each? Is it not possible to think of them as parcels of one fundamental though unformulated truth, different expressions of the same basic principle? Should they then be regarded as members of a more encompassing family? And what is precisely their interrelationship, not in theory, but in practice? Should we think in terms of stages of development in the individual, one method or another being the appropriate one to his station, or is suitability a truly individual matter? These questions are of equal interest to the theorist, the therapist-educator, the institutions concerned with health, education, or welfare, and to the individual who must find his own way.

It is obvious that any attempt at evaluating the varied approaches would first require an understanding of the level and the significance of different methods in the process of human development. The theoretical formulations of different psychological schools provide a rationale for a specific set of tools which are characteristic of that particular approach, but an all-encompassing format has not been found. We have a chaos and we need a system; we have a bagful of techniques and we need a science of human growth in which these techniques can

* But I will sometimes use the single word *ways* instead of either the longer expression *ways of growth* or the Oriental term *sadhana*.

be employed. This book is an attempt to contribute to such an understanding. Its goal is to find unity in multiplicity and from this perspective to show the many ways to the Great Way of Man. A personal conviction of the author runs throughout its pages: that each one of the psychological schools, methods, or techniques with which he is dealing arose and continues to exist because of its relevance to the *one* central purpose, be it explicit or implicit.

Synthetic contributions have been made at the theoretical level, both in the secular and religious domain. Only twenty years ago fanaticism and competitiveness were much greater among psychotherapists of different schools and followers of different religious creeds than they are now. But since the notion of a basic unity of religious experience is no longer tabooed severely, and since a theory of psychotherapy is emerging beyond particular schools, the time is right for another step: synthesis at the level of method and technique. We can now translate what comparative religion was at the beginning of the century, or what eclectic psychologizing has been in recent years, from the domain of ideas to that of psychological practice. Are the ways of religious guides throughout the world as different from one another as their verbal formulations? In some therapeutic systems we know this is not the case.[8] And when we are in the presence of different ways, is it possible that these may be understood as alternative applications of the same principle, just as different symbols or concepts may stand for a similar experience? In previous generations the attachment to forms would have made such an enterprise hardly acceptable, while now it falls in line with our thirst for essences, the animating forces behind the forms which the forms may reveal—and also conceal.

My involvement with defining this process of unification

began in 1968, when I had the privilege of being chosen as a member of a team that was commissioned by the Educational Policy Research Center* to carry out an investigation of the ways.

Professor Willis Harman, Director of the EPRC, foresees that education may have to undergo a radical shift in emphasis. He also feels that in the domain of psychospiritual technology there is a wealth from which the schools of tomorrow may borrow. But exactly what is there, and how can it be used? Would it be a question of incorporating into the school system this or that particular method among the many? Or should we strive to understand the basic principles underlying the many ways and with knowledge of these principles create the appropriate form? The latter proposition is equivalent to that of attempting to create a unified science of human development; a synthesis more comprehensive than one particular method suitable only to a specific time and people.

Dr. Harman thought that certain effective commonalities might be found among the ways of growth. He hoped that an examination of the actual practice of different schools and traditions would reveal the recurrence of certain techniques, strategies, and recommended attitudes which might be separated from their traditional contexts. This was the basis of our study of modes and methods for the actualization of human potential.

Out of more than one hundred fifty approaches classified into provisional categories, a subsample of sixty was selected for more intensive study. Some of the ways chosen were recent developments: sensitivity-training groups, structural integration, Gestalt therapy, Synectics, bioenergetic analysis; others could be called classical: hatha yoga, tai chi chuan, za-zen;

* The EPRC is part of Stanford Research Institute, and is under contract to the U. S. Department of Education.

still others can be regarded as variations on methods known at all times: progressive relaxation, autogenic training, improvisational theater, psychedelic therapy, and so on. Though the approaches had originated in fields as different from one another as the martial arts of the Far East, the practice of business administration, psychotherapy, and drama, what all these methods had in common was their potential value in the face of a broad conception of the educational endeavor.

For the purpose of analyzing each approach a fact sheet was filled out in which most of the questions converged upon the answers to three basic queries:

1. What is the stated rationale and objective?

2. What are the pedagogy, techniques, and procedures applied?

3. What is experienced? (Among other things, the answer to this question involved a compilation of relevant bibliographic material and obtaining of personal reports from individuals undergoing the various disciplines.)

This material, complemented by our own respective professional backgrounds and personal experience, served as a systematic basis for our task.

My particular role in the analysis proper was to examine the various ways from the phenomenological or experiential point of view. A behavioral approach to the question of similarities between the systems, in the form of a reductive analysis of the techniques, was the undertaking of Dr. John Mann. My personal bias is that it is in the domain of experience rather than in that of behavior that the unity between the different systems can be seen most distinctly and approached most directly. Experience constitutes the actual locus of significant commonalities, the domain of convergence. The kind of change involved in personal evolution is essentially a change in attitudes, points of view, ways of experiencing the world.

Though all kinds of conditioning or programing of behavior are conceivable, the type that is involved in the developmental approaches lies not in a conditioning to this or that response but in a qualitative change of being.* To understand this subtle developmental process the experiential or phenomenological approach is in my opinion the most legitimate and appropriate.

The invitation to take part in the Education Policy Research Center project coincided with my own need to give expression to what I might call my then implicit eclecticism. As a part of my formation as a psychiatrist and human being I have been exposed to a rather large number of psychological and spiritual exercises: from my original background of psychoanalysis to encounter groups, from meditation to religious rituals, from structural integration to Indonesian dancing. Whatever the quality of my work in any particular field, I have been a person of wide interests who always had difficulty in giving up any particular one. I have, therefore, led for years a triple life of psychotherapist, musician, and student of religion. Disparate as my activities have seemed to my friends, I have always felt that I am basically doing not different things but the same one in different ways; more precisely, I feel that I have always been seeking the same thing. In recent years, I have also become aware that I have reaped the same thing; all my efforts have been like different ingredients for the same product or roads to the same place. What search? What product? What place?

There is an Oriental story† that tells how four travelers—a Persian, a Turk, an Arab, and a Greek—were debating how to spend the last coin that they had left. "I want *angur*," said the

* Paradoxically, this does not imply that conditioning methods are completely out of place among the ways of growth, as will be discussed in Chapter IV.

† I am borrowing the story from Idries Shah's *The Sufis*.

Persian, but the Turk insisted that *uzum* was what he wanted, while the Arab argued for *inab,* and the Greek for *stafil.* A man came along, and, hearing their heated discussion, offered to buy what each wanted if they would only agree to give him the coin. The men distrusted him at first, but finally agreed. When the passerby, who was a linguist, bought a small bunch of grapes for each of them, the Persian, the Turk, the Arab, and the Greek were surprised and delighted to receive their *angur-uzum-inab-stafil.*[9]

We all want the same thing, the story seems to say, but we call it different names: love, achievement, religion, healing . . . and have correspondingly different ideas as to where to find it. Most men spend much of their energy arguing for the virtue of their own interpretation, and never get to eat the grapes unless a linguist appears. And linguists—men who know *what* words mean—are a rare type of man. I think that I have spent much time in the past letting the travelers within me waste precious time in arguing. I must have developed a slight linguistic ability by now, since I realize that this had been the case, and I feel less hungry. And most relevant to my undertaking in these pages is that I see that two fields of activity which I once regarded as different compartments of my life—the quest for healing and the quest for enlightenment—have merged in my experience to the point of becoming like the upper and lower registers of a single musical instrument.

It should be understandable then that in my approach to psychotherapy I found myself using all that I had learned from life, not feeling comfortable or "right" in adhering strictly to a single technique for healing. At first, I reprimanded myself for lack of discipline, but later came to sense that I was adhering strictly to a very precise view of things, though this was an implicit one that I was not able to formulate as a whole.

My notion of a pattern of "rightness" into which all techniques fitted was enhanced by a sense of resonance with highly evolved persons that I have known. Although they were extremely individualized beings, each with his own style, I felt as if they all acted out of the same unformulated master plan or world view. I sensed a kinship and basic agreement among these men even though they sometimes disagreed, and I knew that what accord there was between them arose from within and not from without: from a quality of experience and not from reading the same books. Even when their reactions were different, it was as if they were acting upon the same laws, as pilots maneuvering differently but always within the conditions set by gravity and by the function of their planes. Or, putting it differently, though they might take separate routes, I believe that they were using the same map.

Imagine that you could see cars circulating in a city without being able to see the city itself, its streets or its buildings. If you watched a number of cars you might notice that they were taking different routes, but not altogether. Even though their points of departure and arrival would generally be different, you would find that at times their paths overlapped. When their origin and destination happened to be the same, there still might be an individual style in their choice of route, but the overlap would tend to increase. On the other hand, you would notice that a car would never cross certain areas or go in certain directions—areas which you are not aware are occupied by houses, and directions which you are not aware are those of the streets and avenues. If you watched the traffic closely for a long time, you would be able to infer the map of the city—a map that all drivers would be respecting, intentionally or not.

This metaphor does not always apply to psychotherapists and gurus, for psychotherapists and gurus do not necessarily know that they are in the same city as their fellow guides. Each one of them believes that his map is a private one (and the best), as he does not recognize that it is but one variation of a master map or one portion that overlaps the other sections.

My belief in the master map is not entirely based on inference. I might say that I have *seen* the map on occasions, or seen glimpses of some quarters, and noticed how they run into one another. In these moments I have seen connections between different psychotherapeutic or cognate resources that I know, and I have even felt that they are the same thing under different guises. When this has happened—moments of B-cognition as Maslow would call them—I understood the relevance of the approaches I know to a more encompassing whole. But these are fleeting moments, and like an astronaut crossing a new space without a camera I have been left with only fragmentary notes, with only partial memory of connections, in a world where everything is interconnected. I want to remember more of these glimpses. Most of the time I do not know what I know, and would like to establish a better communication with the parts of myself that have the answers. (Do we not all have such glimpses?) In terms of this desire, few tasks could have been more appealing than that of looking at the ways of growth as I have done in the following chapters. In making my implicit views explicit I make my self explicit to myself.

I am sorry to say that I am not ready to offer the complete map and wonder whether anyone ever will. But this writing is at least done from the point of view of the map. I have dealt with the ways of growth from the perspective of the whole. This consolidates my own grasp of wholeness, and I hope that it may do the same for others.

Unity of Cultural Forms

The present attempt at a synthesis of education and ways of growth overlaps with the convergence of different institutions and aspects of a culture. Out of the desire for grapes men have carried out a number of activities quite dissimilar in appearance, such as collecting manure to fertilize the vines, building means of transportation to the vineyards, and earning money to buy the treasured fruit from others. In the real situation of our culture, matters are complicated by the fact that many of the activities which originated in appreciation of grapes are now carried out mechanically, just because our ancestors did them, just because that is what they taught us to do and what we are used to doing, or because everyone else does the same.

There is reason to argue, for instance, that morality had its historical sources in an enlightened perception of certain ways of life thought to be conducive to man's development in a given community and time, and that it was not merely the outcome of a compromise between economic needs, individual desires, and superstition. At its fountainhead, morality is far from being what it has come to be in the course of history, i.e., an aspect of an authoritarian conception of the place of man in the world, wherein certain things become a must for themselves—an absolute good rather than a good-for-man.

Culture, of course, is more than the use to which men have put their leisure time when not engaged in the serious business of surviving. Nor is it the style adopted by men for the solution of survival problems. History gives us ample evidence that in all the great cultures men regarded themselves as living *for* something. "Culture" was one of the things for which man lived. But our culture is now only a pale reflection of a grape-producing system, an awkward mimicry of the agricultural instruments required for true results. No wonder that fewer and fewer men feel inclined to die for its values.

The study of the history of culture can help us understand how a particular sphere of activity may relate to that which Tillich calls "ultimate concern." The administration of justice, for instance—a matter which is perceived today as no more than a convenient solution to conflict—was seen through the eyes of the Israelites at the time of the Judges as an activity that epitomized man's relationship to God: the interpretation of His Law. The executive function in government can be similarly seen as related to the question of ultimate concern in examples ranging from Plato's conception of government to Mohammed's, and to Gandhi's personal example of government in this century. In the Dervish tradition, crafts, which are to most of the world a mere tribute to Caesar, are elevated to an important function in the process of spiritual guidance and unfoldment (by the manner, context, and attitude in which they are carried out)—again a matter of "ultimate concern," or "grapes." Many examples could be cited: the case of sports and the Japanese martial arts, storytelling among some American Indian tribes, and so forth. But we do not grow up with the exemplar, or even the utopian dream of a culture, in which every limb is animated by man's ultimate purpose. That purpose forgotten, we see its reflections in different aspects: entertainment, pleasure, beauty, edification, duty, usefulness, love, worship, and so on. Each of these cultural forms contains a number of words for "grapes" with which this book is particularly concerned: from the religious domain, salvation, deliverance, enlightenment, liberation, self-realization; from the psychotherapeutic, healing, maturing, achieving balance, authenticity, self-actualization, full-humanness. In this book, I have systematically tried to show how these two cultural domains merge on certain basic goals. Less consistently have I shown the relevance of art to the same issues, and less consistently still, the bearing upon these of social and practical life in general. Precisely because the matter of integrating cultural domains is something that I have not worked out in detail and left somewhat implicit, I am stressing the issue in this first chapter.

As well as being a book on psychotherapeutic and religious issues, this is a book about education—yet I say little about education in particular. This is because I regard everything as a statement about education. Education is not only "one more" domain of culture, but a microcosm of them all. Education is culture being passed on—and is inseparable from culture's very nature. Education only becomes an independent field of endeavor to the extent that it becomes the art or science of deliberate transmission of cultural attainments. Even in this sense, the whole of this book is about education: its subject matter is the intentional transmission of culture, in the essential meaning of the word.

Too often we forget that culture is a matter of culturing or cultivation, and that it has the same origin as the word agriculture. Culture is not something that we can have, but something that we are: We are cultivated to the extent that we have grown up. Similarly, to cultivate is to grow people. But we lose sight of the intrinsic sense of culture, we misinterpret the growth process as the acquisition of traits or attributes borrowed from without. Then we must take culture for something added to the person, a *possession* rather than a *quality* of the mind.

When we do this, education also becomes an extrinsic education: a handing over of forms (conceptual, attitudinal, behavioral) which may have originated in cultivated beings or may be used as tools for cultivation by one who knows how, but which only superficially may be equated with culture.

This is a time when we are abandoning forms and searching for the essence that animates them, an essence which often lies hidden in the forms themselves. Thus we are also on the brink of a deformalization of education: a reconsideration of its nature and goal, in which we come to understand again its essence as that of transmitting an essence. Forms were means that came to be worshiped as ends, and the old means are likely to be superseded. The ways of growth that have originated in fields other than that of formal education are likely to provide a number of resources for the future development of human beings.

Principally, though, I believe that we will acknowledge more and more that means are not all that is needed to attain the ends: as life proceeds from life, human growth is self-duplicating like the chromosome; true culture transmits itself without much need for an educational technology. Techniques are situations and locations that make the transmission more likely or possible, but _what_ is transmitted is a condition of being. Furthermore, "transmission" is only a manner of speech: nothing is transmitted; rather, the more evolved human being catalyzes the growth of the less evolved.

To the extent that we come to see cultural transmission as a chain of effects of more "cultivated" beings upon less "cultivated" rather than just the passing on of habits and information, we will lay more stress on the development of teachers as human beings rather than on the things that children should learn. Maybe we will come to trust that education takes care of itself if we take care of ourselves.

What This Book Is Not

After stating what this book deals with, I want to specify what is not a part of its purpose.

It is a work of theory and general ideas—not one of description. The reader interested in detailed information or in the specific methods mentioned should refer to the relevant sources. For this purpose bibliographic indications are provided at the end of the book.

It is a work of expression of ideas rather than one of demonstration. In it, I have sought to share certain thoughts or points of view which might be inspiring, useful, or enlightening. I am letting them stand on their own worth without trying to prove every point by detailed argument and documentation. Quotations are given with the objective of clarification, of imparting some taste of the texts dealing with the different methods discussed, and to give the reader some respite from my homogeneous style.

It is not a book of evaluation. This does not mean that I do not have opinions of the relative merits of different systems or groups, but that I have chosen not to share them in this context. I have been concerned with principles rather than judgments. I hope that these may provide some basis for evaluation, in that they can contribute toward the appreciation of what deserves to be appreciated. In that sense the book may be considered a work of criticism though only in the positive sense of the term. Just as an art critic may contribute toward the understanding of a masterpiece through an insightful commentary or exegesis, I think that I may be contributing toward the building of a bridge between the intent of certain pursuits and their popular misunderstandings. I am aware of a need for orientation in the individual who seeks something that many ways offer but who does not know how to choose. The factor which would determine such practical choices, though, is rarely the value of a method, but the understanding and quality of the persons who represent it; the best musical instrument fails to produce good music in the hands of a poor musician.

There is more or less truth in all the ways, but this is coun-teracted by the limitations within which they are framed: lim-itations of the system itself, sometimes, but mostly limitations in the attitude with which they are applied. Their factor of error is in what they deny more than in what they affirm, in what they inhibit rather than in what they do. Much of the blocking effect of many paths derives from the very fact of their promising too much. Thus they create an addiction to a hope or a dream rather than allowing for a realistic appraisal of what is being accomplished. Promises which are manifested as limiting dogmatism stem from the investment of self-esteem on the part of groups and pseudohelpers or from their need to hold on to their own dreams by having others share them and confirm them. Aside from the words "Beware of fanatics, pros-elytizers, and con men" I know of no effective antidote to this. In growth relationships, as in friendship or marriage, each gets what he deserves.

Another aspect in the individual's choice among the ways is that of personal suitability, in terms of his unique structure and stage of development. This is also a matter where general statements cannot help. An expert may be able to prescribe in a particular case, but unfortunately experts with a broad per-spective of alternatives are rare. The only solution that I see to this problem is in the refinement of the individual's selectivity and in the availability of opportunities to exercise it. This means the availability of many ways in an unbiased environ-ment: the chance to taste and the freedom to decide. In our culture both conditions are now present to a larger extent than ever before.

THE GOALS OF HUMAN TRANSFORMATION

The philosophers, logicians and doctors of law were drawn up at Court to examine Nasrudin. This was a serious case, because he had admitted going from village to village saying: "The so-called wise men are ignorant, irresolute and confused." He was charged with undermining the security of the State.

"You may speak first," said the King.

"Have paper and pens brought," said the Mulla.

Paper and pens were brought.

"Give some to each of the first seven savants."

They were distributed.

"Have them separately write an answer to this question: 'What is bread?'"

This was done.

The papers were handed to the King, who read them out:

The first said: "Bread is a food."

The second: "It is flour and water."

The third: "A gift of God."

The fourth: "Baked dough."

The fifth: "Changeable, according to how you mean 'bread'."

The sixth: "A nutritious substance."

The seventh: "Nobody really knows."

"When they decide what bread is," said Nasrudin, "it will be possible for them to decide other things. For example, whether I am right or wrong. Can you entrust matters of assessment and judgment to people like this? Is it or is it not strange that they cannot agree about something which they eat each day, yet are unanimous that I am a heretic?"

—From *The Exploits of the Incomparable Mulla Nasrudin.*[1]

To but one goal are marching everywhere
All human beings, though they may seem to walk
Divergent paths; and that Goal is I.

—From the *Bhagavad-Gita*[2]

Three institutions are overtly concerned with eliciting change or facilitating a change process in the minds and behavior of human beings: education, medicine, and religion. The nature of the change process that is the focus of each may at first glance seem quite specific to the institution: *development* being the province of education, *healing* that of medicine, and *salvation, liberation,* or *enlightenment* that of religion. Yet, the three were one in the past—when the shaman or primitive mystic was a medicine man, a wise man, a counselor, an initiator, and an artist. Today we seem to be rediscovering the unity of "ultimate concern" beyond the temporal purposes and the irrelevant concerns of education, psychiatry, and religion. Indeed, if we examine closely the nature of the separate quests for growth, sanity, and enlightenment, we may discover enough of a meeting ground among them to warrant the ambition of a unified science and art of human change. Since this book is in the nature of a contribution toward that goal and cuts across the different domains of endeavor that have given rise to the various ways of growth, we may do well to show some aspects of the commonality that exists among their aims. It is a commonality too often forgotten when we think of their specific means, fields of application, and terminologies.

The Goal of Education

Let us first take the notion of development, the goal of education. Implicit in the art of education is the belief in a spontaneous growth process that may be influenced by environmental conditions. Just as the body needs nourishment and vitamins, exercise, and a certain amount of protection to survive and develop into what it can potentially become, the mind too needs its proper food, exercise, and care.

To become what? Here the discrepancies begin. If the answer is "what it can potentially become," we have a humanistic approach in the true sense of making man the measure: to each according to his individual goals and inclinations. Education becomes the task of giving each individual what he thirsts for, without any attempt to mold him into a pre-established pattern. Just as a gardener trusts that the shape of every plant will proceed from within if he only provides it with the optimum conditions, the educator believes in the innate goodness of man and sees himself as an aid to this intrinsic growth process.

The very word *education* contains the notion of a development of the person from within. The Latin *educare* derives from *educere,* "to extract or lead forth, to draw out something hidden or enclosed into the open." The conception implied in this etymology is that of the human being as engaged in a *growth process* that may be facilitated by the agency of others.

Needless to say, we are here speaking of an approach that probably cannot be found in pure form in reality, just as a perfect circle cannot be found outside the world of ideas. We can find it as a component of education in general though, and in some instances as its major component, as in A. S. Neill's *Summerhill*,[3] in the Montessori approach,[4] or in the example of Pestalozzi, who inspired so much of the educational re-evaluation of this century. The following lines of this Swiss educator are as explicit as any statement about an inner-directed growth process:

> Sound Education stands before me symbolized by a tree planted near fertilizing water. A little seed, which contains the design of the tree, its form and proportion, is placed in the soil. See how it germinates and expands into trunk, branches, leaves, flowers, and fruit! The whole tree is an uninterrupted chain of organic parts, the plan of which existed in its seed and root. Man is similar to the tree. In the newborn child are hidden those faculties which are to unfold during life.[5]

A belief in the self-regulation of the organism—including the psyche—has grown steadily in the pyschology of the last three decades or so. The old view of man as an intrinsically amoral or evil being who needs to be brainwashed is being superseded by another that sees man as a self-actualizing being, and I believe that this view is flowing in part from psychology into the culture at large.

In the domain of religion the notion of an unfolding from within is found in every great tradition, though it is often obscured by the authoritarian structures (and rationalizations) of religious institutions. For instance, in Zen, we see the trust in the Buddha nature within each creature which in essence is no different from the Christian's vision of himself as a prodigal son of the Heavenly King, destined to return to His Kingdom. The difference in this case is principally one of emphasis, for the Christian notion has become a purely theoretical one, while in Mahayana Buddhism we find a living attitude of trust in the workings of the universe. How this type of attitude has generated specific ways of growth is something that we will have occasion to examine in the following chapters.

In contrast to the open-ended, humanistic view of man's development, seen as a fulfillment of man's inner trend, is any pre-established view of what man's end is, of where his unfolding leads, and of what his most desirable state of being is. The answers to these questions have been the concern of philosophers and prophets through the ages, and as Aldous Huxley has attempted to show in his *Perennial Philosophy*[6] their answers are not as different as might be expected. Beyond culture-bound notions of right and wrong, the wise ones of all lands throughout history seem to agree as to the existence of a *way* or *path* leading to man's fulfillment and the finding of his true place in the world, not according to a theoretical construction but as a realization. According to such views the development of a child is but a first stage in a long developmental process the end of which may well not be attained within an individual's lifetime.

Those who share this positive conception of man's destiny see the first stages of life as not only the natural time for the beginning of his evolution, but also as the time of his thwarting. In both religion and psychiatry we find, along with the exposition of ideals, a pervasive awareness that man's reality falls short of such ideals, and a lamentation that during his formative years of life a person not only fails to develop but is distorted by pressures in his environment.

The bearing of this perspective on a conception of human development is that, once we regard man as straying from his path because of his social conditioning, we can discriminate between two phases in the journey toward the desirable goal: the treading of the path and, before that, the process of finding it. The development of the child as it actually proceeds is thus seen as a thwarting of his true direction in the midst of a culturally disturbed environment. Consequently, a conversion will be necessary to reorient his life in view of the true path, a "death" to his outward nature, a renunciation or separation (as in Christ's "And a man's foes shall be they of his own household"), or an awakening. Such notions are inseparable from the mythical accounts in all religions of the fall of man, for the condition of fallen man—humanity—is that of "sin," "illusion," "sleep," "blindness," and his first aim is that of undoing his "fall."

Thus, the first stage in the attainment of spiritual fullness according to Taoism is to become a "true man"; only after this, can man become a "universal man." In Sufism, too, we find the notion of two successive stages in a developmental process, the first of which is in the nature of reowning something that was forgotten or lost. The notion of "forgetting" a higher world is so important in Plato's philosophy that even the word he uses for "truth" (a-letheia) means no-forgetting. And in the poetic monument of Christianity, Dante's *Commedia*, two stages of attainment are depicted. In the first, man reaches "earthly paradise," his original abode. Here he is healed, and Dante says of himself:

> I came back from those holiest waters new, remade, reborn, like a sun-wakened tree that spreads new foliage to the spring dew in sweet freshness, healed of winter's scars; perfect, pure, and ready for the Stars.[7]

Beyond this, a man can still venture into "Paradise," a world of transcendence, where he experiences a unity with the cosmos as conceived of by religious thought.

Just as in religion we find that the ideas of a corrective and of a maturational process go hand in hand (the *via purgativa* and *via unitiva* of Christianity), in psychology too we find acknowledgment of a need for corrective work and of a developmental process that may take place when not unnaturally obstructed. In other words, psychiatry and psychology share with the religious view both the notion of a wrongness in the condition of average humanity and that of a developmental process that goes much beyond the school years. In the terms of dynamic psychology, the process of maturation has been arrested in childhood years and much of the psychotherapeutic process amounts to a liberation from childish fixations or blocks to growth. Furthermore, psychology has moved more and more in the direction of seeing an aim beyond that of healing. Beyond the correction of a wrongness the psychotherapist has come to recognize the existence of a void that needs to be filled, an urge for more that his patient wants to satisfy and that cannot be fulfilled by material ambitions, by his family life, or his work. The answers to such a challenge vary, so that Frankl speaks of search for meaning and logotherapy, Jung speaks of analytical psychology as the modern process of initiation,* and Maslow points out that the peak-experiences most people have during their lifetimes indicate the possibility of a more satisfactory way of being which is impeded by unfulfilled basic needs such as those for safety, love, and respect. Healing, according to these authors, falls short of making a man complete or mature in more than a conventional sense; its nature is that of liberating him to his essential concern which is precisely that of further growth. The religious notions of a *way* or *path, Tao,* and *dharma* find an echo in some contemporary psychological formulations such as that of the self-actualizing drive of the organism (Goldstein) or Jung's description of the individuation process.

* See quotation, pp. 139 ff.

As the history of education amply shows, the danger of an educational approach that has in view a preconceived notion of man's goal is in its potential rigidity. In this, as in other fields, a truth that is learned and repeated is not a truth any more but a mechanical act. A statement of man's desirable goal or path may very well be accurate and yet there is a difference between intellectual statements and the understanding that can lead to the application of a truth. Without such understanding, all systems can become ways of thwarting the development that they want to foster.

How much of what we call education is only a pale shadow of activities that had a purpose long ago? The main trait of contemporary education, for example, is its emphasis upon amassing information. This trend received its impetus in the Renaissance, when men turned to a forgotten antiquity in their thirst for wisdom, and the acquisition of wisdom came to be seen as inseparable from understanding the writings of Greek and Latin classics. At first there was sense in this expression of humanism, and we may grant Erasmus that he was still thinking functionally when he designed a method of teaching that would make the child into a Greek and Latin scholar and a pious man. He was no Ciceronian: Latin was to be taught so as to be of use. And, most important of all, he saw that education would have to follow nature to achieve the best results.

But it seems to be a law of history that every good becomes an ought, every God an idol, every meaningful practice an empty ritual. It was perhaps the influence of Sturm, above that of any other single individual, that was responsible for the transition leading from true humanism to the gentleman's polite tipping of the hat. As the tutor of Queen Elizabeth and first great headmaster, he has been regarded as the introducer of "scholarship" into the schools. The means that once served the purpose of human development came more and more to be pursued as ends in themselves; what were tools of certain tasks became objects of worship; and scholarship turned into an imitation derived from what once was learning as a means to deeper understanding. As the contents of scholarship changed with the years, science and history took the place of the classics, but the attitude remained the same: learning things had become the goal of education and taken the place of self-understanding. Learning things for what? The question was never pursued too far; nor was it demonstrated that this was "to train the mind" or "prepare for life."

We could draw a parallel here between the two approaches to human development and parental love, as described by Erich Fromm.[8] The unconditional mother's love finds its parallel in the first (inner-directed) approach, trusting and unconditional; the demanding father's love corresponds to the second (outer-directed) approach, which guides the individual toward the highest ideals. The balance between these two approaches is always an inescapable issue in the educational process. It is a balance between the individual and tradition, the unknown and the known, creativity and the wisdom of the ages.

There is still a third "answer" to the goal of human development, more implicit than explicit, even though, for this very reason, it is perhaps the most powerful. The goal of this third approach to education is neither that chosen by the individual nor that inspired by tradition, but consists in the adaptation of the individual to the habitual (or modal) way of being in a given culture. Just as the humanistic attitude trusts and encourages the development of feelings and the idealistic approach is predominantly intellectual, this third attitude may be regarded as predominantly mechanistic. Not only does a child mechanically imitate what he sees and hears, from language and gait to personality styles, but much of his socialization process consists of the positive and negative reinforcement that he receives in terms of what adults like. Behind each command or prohibition there is an implicit statement of "this is right" which most often does not stem from thinking or decision but from having been exposed to the same dogma in earlier years. Thus, it is right to use the fingers in eating in India but not in England; it is right for an Eskimo to share his wife on occasion but not for a Jivaro Indian; it is right to be future-oriented in the United States today but not in present-oriented areas of Mexico or tradition-oriented circles in Japan. Regardless of what may actually be right in terms of human needs, there are societal notions of what is right, the obvious rationalization of a process of conditioning. The source of the cultural traits that are thus transmitted may be in an ideal that became automatized, in economic circumstances, or in the emotional needs of parents. A child's demand for affection, for instance, may give rise to guilt feelings in parents who are falling short of filling his need and cause them to say that it is not nice to cry, that grownups do not complain, etc., and thus contribute to the perpetuation of traits of both independence and affectlessness.

The pervasiveness of the socialization process cannot fail to color the educational endeavor, and it may even become a goal of education to produce the kind of "people that the country needs." Yet this molding process should not be really considered as an approach—adequate or not—to development, but rather as an "impurity" in the approach itself. Conditioning does not posit a growth process or anything like a "human nature." Its goals are those of convenience, its ways may be ways of change but are not ways of growth. This does not exclude that principles of conditioning may be used in the service of human development, as we point out in Chapter IV, but such use generally takes the form of a deconditioning ("desensitization") that allows for increased flexibility and choice, and a reinforcement of the natural developmental process until it is experienced as self-rewarding. This is how behaviorists currently interpret psychoanalysis and client-centered therapy, in which the therapist encourages the act of self-disclosure and expression.

Though the notion of development is the concern of education more than of any other institution, it is also a core concept in religion, when we reach for the true significance of this term, and in psychiatry and psychology.

The Goal of Psychotherapy

The idea of psychological disease was at first a purely descriptive one, defined by the presence of certain symptoms. Later it became a statistical notion according to which "neuroticism" or even "psychoticism" are present in some degree in everybody. Furthermore, psychological disease became divorced from its external signs or symptoms. Thus in dynamic psychology a neurotic personality or action is judged from the point of view of its motivation rather than from its behavioral reality or even the individual's subjective state of well-being or discomfort at the moment. Also, in reaching for a deeper understanding of neuroticism, psychiatry has become more and more concerned with matters such as authenticity and estrangement, the real self, responsibility, and other issues that were formerly the concern of philosophy or religions. In fact, what psychiatry is presently doing is not just curing physical or emotional symptoms of psychic origin, but helping the individual to find the good life for himself—as philosophy and religion had been doing for centuries, prior to becoming riddled with abstract speculation and authoritarian dogma.

Just as psychiatry today tends to see symptoms as the outer manifestation of the failure to meet life with the right attitude, religions at the time of their greatest aliveness have seen man's behavioral and moral shortcomings as outward expressions of his original sin which is not essentially a moral but a spiritual mistake and is a disease, a source of suffering. *Salvation* comes from the Latin *salvare* which has the same root as the word *salus* (health, safety); in French too, *salut* (salvation) comes from the Latin *salus*. The same connection is seen in the German *heilig* (holy, saintly) and *heilen* (to heal). In the Old Testament and in rabbinical literature, sin is frequently described as folly or madness. In Buddhism, too, the question is one of deliverance from the suffering that man experiences as a result of his ignorance, a condition which is indifferently called sin or disease.

Regardless of whether we accept the formulations of psychiatry or of religion, one thing is clear: the recognition of the interrelatedness of physical and moral health or illness. Psychiatry today stresses the inability to cope with certain moral issues (i.e., responsibility, perception of values, genuineness) as the sources of psychological or psychosomatic symptoms. And both psychology and religion, in different terms, have also pointed out the cognitive issues at the root of the moral ones: understanding, consciousness, awareness of real attunement to the truth.

However, there is apparently no consensus among present-day psychiatrists or psychologists as to the boundaries of "mental disease" or its defining criteria. The concepts of different schools still range from the strictly symptomatic one of *dis-ease* to those of humanistic or dynamic psychology. It is to the former, restricted sense of disease and sanity that Thomas Merton is referring in the following paragraphs from "A Devout Meditation in Memory of Adolph Eichmann."

One of the most disturbing facts that came out in the Eichmann trial was that a psychiatrist examined him and pronounced him *perfectly sane.* I do not doubt it at all, and that is precisely why I find it disturbing.

If all the Nazis had been psychotics, as some of their leaders probably were, their appalling cruelty would have been in some sense easier to understand. It is much worse to consider this calm, "well-balanced," unperturbed official conscientiously going about his desk work, his administrative job which happened to be the supervision of mass murder. He was thoughtful, orderly, unimaginative. He had a profound respect for system, law and order. He was obedient, loyal, a faithful officer of a great state. He served his government very well.

He was not bothered much by guilt. I have not heard that he developed any psychosomatic illnesses. Apparently, he slept well. He had a good appetite, or so it seems.

And later in the same essay:

I am beginning to realize that "sanity" is no longer a value or an end in itself. The "sanity" of modern man is about as useful to him as the huge bulk and muscles of the dinosaur. If he were a little less sane, a little more doubtful, a little more aware of his absurdities and contradictions, perhaps there might be a possibility of his survival. But if he is sane, too sane . . . perhaps we must say that in a society like ours the worst insanity is totally without anxiety, totally "sane." [9]

Contrast the view of mental disease in the above quotation to that presented in the following passage by a psychiatrist:

. . . Let us begin with a very extreme case. Let us take for instance, one of advanced senile dementia. Why does everyone agree to regard such a person diseased? What first strikes us is the loss of his essential psychological faculties; he cannot do what others can do; he cannot, for instance, orient himself in time or space, attend to his physiologic needs, control his sphincters, and so on. Yet it is clear that such an individual is not considered to be sick merely because he cannot fulfill such functions, for if this were the case, an infant would have to be considered just as diseased. What is pathological here is not his inability but inability where we would expect ability.

After considering other instances, this author concludes that:

We always evaluate an individual's psychological activity in terms of his optimal potential, and do not regard as mentally ill he who behaves in this or that manner, but him whose optimal potential for performance is altered from within. In other words, his potentialities are prevented their full unfolding because they are hindered from within and in spite of himself, so that they are thwarted and deviated from full expression.[10]

According to such a view the notion of mental disease becomes correlative to our understanding of man's potential, for only in terms of the latter can we say whether an individual is falling short of his optimal functioning. So at this point a medical conception becomes inseparable from a conception of man's nature, man's purpose and destiny, and particularly the direction and goal of his development. In fact, the issues of health and development, the concerns of medicine and education, become one.

It would seem that the existential and ever-present foundation of the quests for both healing and enlightenment is in a dissatisfaction on the part of a fraction of humanity, a thirst that cannot be quenched by objective achievements. A traditional psychiatrist would look upon such an urge as abnormal and think, "Here is a person who cannot enjoy the given and is therefore unsatisfied. He must be cured of his inability to enjoy to the fullest." From the religious, spiritual, or esoteric point of view, the same person may be regarded instead as one who is no more sick (or removed from God, divided from his deeper self, etc.) than average humanity, but who has not become anesthetized to his suffering. Just as physical pain signals a physical damage, psychological distress may be taken as the functional signal of a psychological wrongness, and many a neurotic may be simply more awake to the problem than a completely automatized, "adjusted" human being.

The individual, too, may interpret his own urge according to different alternatives presented by the culture and feel, for instance:

"I lack something, I feel unfulfilled, empty; I should study, acquire a wider culture and understanding of things, or travel, and then I would feel satisfied."

"I lack something, my life is not rich enough; I know the answer is in love. I have not found somebody to whom I can give all my love, and who loves me. Warmth and caring is what is missing from life."

"I lack something, I feel unfulfilled. Nothing that I do or acquire will give me the sense of fulfillment that I seek; this I know from experience. The answer lies in myself. I am very far from God. I have been neglecting the inner quest, forgetting that this is what I really want."

"I lack something. No matter what I do, I feel unfulfilled and empty. Is this what psychiatrists call depression, or perhaps neurasthenia, or simple schizophrenia? I should do something about myself, and go into treatment."

The last two answers are similar, in that the dissatisfaction is interpreted as a sign of the pursuit of inner change, but they differ in that one is cast in religious language and the other in medical or psychological terms. The difference between the religious and the psychological interpretations of dissatisfaction is not that between a theistic and an atheistic view, as typically evidenced by atheistic religions (such as Buddhism or Taoism). The difference lies more in the relative stress on the ideas of lack and wrongness. The urge directing the quest for enlightenment is interpreted as a lack of fulfillment, a separation from God or higher faculties, and the process of attainment is frequently depicted as a reaching of another shore, crossing a bridge, climbing up to the heights or down into an abyss. Man's sickness and sins are the outcome of his lack: that of being removed from the presence of God, which he must become conscious of and repair in becoming one with God. Though the concept of disease is that of a wrongness in the organism or mind, in the psychological view, too, man's sickness and its symptoms are the outcome of a lack which different writers have presented in different ways: a lack of consciousness, of self-love, of contact with the real self, etc. Such a lack stems from a "wrong" pattern of psychological functioning that resists being altered and sets up defenses. Whatever language we choose to describe the inner events that are the issue of both psychiatry and religion, we can see that wrongness (illness) and deficit (de-ficiency) are interdependent. For the emptiness to be truly filled, it is necessary first of all that it be acknowledged as emptiness by removing defenses and substitute contents, much as the Zen worker Nan-in indicated to the European university professor who visited him at the turn of the century:

> Nan-in served tea. He poured his visitor's cup full, and then kept on pouring.
>
> The professor watched the overflow until he no longer could restrain himself. "It is overfull. No more will go in!"
>
> "Like this cup," Nan-in said, "you are full of your own opinions and speculations. How can I show you Zen unless you first empty your cup?" [11]

This may be enough to indicate that the concept of mental health, just as the idea of development, is only one element in the understanding of a process of human change that is the common concern of education, medicine, and religion. And just as the practical goal of education represents a compromise between a nurturing of the individual's development and the demands of society, so psychiatry and psychology, too, serve two masters: the individual patient, and the local culture. Also, as in the domain of education we can contrast the view of a development from within and the belief in such a thing as human nature with another view of cultural relativity in which the good can only be defined in terms of the needs of society, so, too, in psychiatry we can discern a developmental view that stresses some constancies in human nature and self-actualization, and another that stresses cultural relativity and the goal of adaptation. It is undoubtedly the latter that has led many humanists and those concerned with the spiritual endeavor to question the relevance of psychiatry to their own interests, and has put the term *head shrinker* in the mouth of many a common man.

The Goal of Religion

Let us now turn our attention to the nature of the religious quest associated with expressions such as salvation, deliverance, enlightenment, union with or rejection of God.

As in psychiatry and in education, we find here many "schools" which differ from one another not so much in their essential goal, but in their symbolic and conceptual language; in the admixture of elements, other than the concern for whatever man's ultimate concern may be, into the complex phenomenon called religion. Even more than in the domains of education and psychotherapy, perhaps, the invisible power of socialization has seized religion, using it for its own end of molding people into conformity. It is because of the local ethical and dogmatic difference in religion that some prefer to speak of mysticism when referring to the common core of religious experience out of which the different religions have sprung. Others speak of mysticism in connection with a particular modality of religious experience and development and use the word *esoteric* in reference to "the transcendent unity of religions." [12] Furthermore, within some religions such as Taoism or Buddhism an esoteric or inner circle is found where the essence of religion and man are the issue, and there are other esoteric groups (of varying authoritativeness and quality) that are not bound to any single "religion."

According to the esoteric tradition, many world religions have originated from a single stream of transmission of living understanding in which their leaders were initiated, a stream which remains independent of each of them and is still alive today.*

Whatever the historical truth concerning the idea of a single stream of teaching behind the diversity of religions, we may still accept the existence of a single stream of meaning and intent beyond the diversity of religious forms. The deterioration of such forms is feelingly expressed in a tale by Ahmed-el-Bedavi (died 1275) who, "according to dervish lore, was accused by Moslems of preaching Christianity but repudiated by Christians because he refused to accept later Christian dogma literally." This is how the story begins, according to the version of Idries Shah:

> Once upon a time a man was contemplating the ways in which Nature operates, and he discovered, because of his concentration and application, how fire could be made.
>
> This man was called Nour. He decided to travel from one community to another, showing people his discovery.

* This idea runs through the books of Guénon,[13] for instance, or from a journalistic point of view, through the pages of Pauwels' *The Dawn of Magic*.[14] Interesting documents concerning a surviving and ever renewed science of man are Lefort's *The Teachers of Gurdjieff*,[15] and Roy Davidson's compilation *Documents on Contemporary Dervish Communities*.[16]

Nour passed the secret to many groups of people. Some took advantage of the knowledge. Others drove him away, thinking that he must be dangerous, before they had time to understand how valuable this discovery could be to them. Finally, a tribe before which he demonstrated became so panic-stricken that they set about him and killed him, being convinced that he was a demon.

Centuries passed. The first tribe which had learned about fire reserved the secret for their priests, who remained in affluence and power while the people froze.

The second tribe forgot the art and worshipped instead the instruments. The third worshipped a likeness of Nour himself, because it was he who had taught them. The fourth retained the story of the making of fire in their legends: some believed them, some did not. The fifth community really did use fire, and this enabled them to be warmed, to cook their food, and to manufacture all kinds of useful articles.

After many, many years, a wise man and a small band of his disciples were travelling through the lands of these tribes. The disciples were amazed at the variety of rituals which they encountered; and one and all said to their teacher: "But all these procedures *are* in fact related to the making of fire, nothing else. We should reform these people!"

The teacher said: "Very well, then. We shall restart our journey. By the end of it, those who survive will know the real problems and how to approach them."

The tale goes on telling the failure of this attempt, tribe after tribe, until the wise man and his disciples returned to the lands "where fire-making was a commonplace and where other preoccupations faced them." There the master said to his disciples:

You have to learn how to teach, for man does not want to be taught. First of all, you will have to teach people how to learn. And before that you have to teach them that there is still something to be learned. They imagine that they are ready to learn.

But they want to learn what they *imagine* is to be learned, not what they have first to learn. When you have learned all this, then you can devise a way to teach. Knowledge without special capacity to teach is not the same as knowledge and capacity.[17]

If "fire-making" is what we are speaking of when we talk of growth-healing-enlightenment, the fable is telling us that many of the concerns of humanity are inspired by it and yet they only mimic or substitute the real accomplishment. We hope that our survey of ways of growth may be as free as possible of such idolatries.

Some of the religious concepts associated with the goal of the human quest are implicitly negative: salvation is salvation from sin, liberation and deliverance imply something to be liberated from, and nirvana (extinction) implies that there is an illusion to be extinguished. Other concepts are positive, like enlightenment, awakening, or union (with the divine). Yet the positive and negative aspects are interdependent, as we have noted earlier in defining the relationship between deficit and wrongness. Thus, enlightenment, according to Buddhism, puts an end to the "three evil roots"—delusion, craving, and hate. Sin, in Judaism, is a rebellion in the face of God's Law (man's duty toward the Law being inherent in the doctrine of God's kingship). And God's Law, behind the six hundred thirteen Commandments delivered unto Moses on Mount Sinai, is one: "Seek the Lord and Live." * It would be futile to attempt to define in a few paragraphs the ineffable goal of religious endeavor, but we can probably agree that in its negative aspects it is closely related to the notions of healing and outgrowing, while in its positive aspect it is in the nature of a growth or ev-

* For a commentary of this, see the chapter entitled "The Torah in Its Aspect of Law" in Schechter's *Aspects of Rabbinic Theology*.[18]

olution of the mind. Indeed, the symbolism of generation and development pervades all religious thought; rebirth, emanation, and the tree of life are only a few examples of the central role held by these symbols.

On the whole, the West has laid greater stress upon the negative formulation of the religious goal—salvation—and, accordingly, Christianity has emphasized the *via purgativa*, purification, and the experience of repentance. The East, on the other hand, has emphasized more the positive aspect of the religious goal—living in the Tao—in attunement with one's nature and one's true place in the cosmos. Enlightenment and full awakening of the intrinsic Buddha nature are concepts of the *via unitiva* rather than of the *via purgativa*. Yet both aspects, at the conceptual as well as the practical level, are really two sides of the same coin.

A realization of the commonality between psychotherapy and religion has had to await a deepening in the understanding of emotional disorders and a "de-dogmatization" in the grasp of religious phenomena. Increased communication with the East has been a factor in the process, as well as the work of those who have expounded the essential unity of religions.* In the present book we are taking for granted the existence of a meeting ground and a common direction of intent among the different formulations though not necessarily implying an identity in the goal, for the ultimate goal of spiritual regeneration—"universal" or "cosmic" man—seems more ambitious than the goal of the minor mysteries and of psychotherapy. And we shall not be mainly concerned in this work with the convergence of theoretical formulations in various streams of thought but with that of the practical ways to the unfolding

* See Bhagavan Das, for instance, and the works of Mircea Eliade. For discussions of the relevance of Eastern disciplines to psychotherapy, the interested reader might refer to Watts,[19] Boss,[20] Fromm,[21] Jacobs,[22] Jung,[23] and Zimmer.[24]

of man which have originated within the different spiritual disciplines, therapeutic schools, and educational approaches.

We have seen both psychotherapy and education as composites of two conflicting attempts, one toward socialization and the other toward liberation of the individual from the ills of his culture. Similarly, in religion we find a discrepancy between the One Quest and the attempt to indoctrinate people into a given cultural pattern—through fear of hell, hope of heaven.

How far "religion" today is from fulfilling the function it purports to serve may be seen in the fact that, despite the convergence of its goals with those of psychotherapy, no piece of psychological research has yet established a positive correlation between "religiosity" and well-being, humanitarianism, or sanity.[25] In view of this, we might consider not using the term "religion" at all for what is commonly regarded as a religious issue, or else restrict "religion" to the degraded cultural forms of the phenomenon and not use it when speaking of the quest for growth. Yet, if we were to do this we should also, for consistency, do the same with the terms "education" and "psychotherapy."

To what extent is our education, for instance, a case of *educere,* a "leading forth" or drawing out?

All three—education, psychotherapy, and religion—at the same time pursue and are hostile to the One Goal of human growth. To the extent that they serve the One God they are one; to the extent that they serve Caesar, they are specialties. Yet, paradoxically, Caesar has the best intentions. If we examine his motives, we find that he also serves God, only with little understanding. His decisions are based upon insights that once constituted wisdom but fail to apply any longer; his institutions are the echo of others that once served their true function.

According to one story, when God created the world and saw that it was good, Satan joined him in his appreciation, and exclaimed, as he gazed from one wonder to another, "It is good! It is good! Let us make it an institution!"

III

TRADITIONAL WAYS
AND CONTEMPORARY ECHOES

Nasrudin was sent by the King to investigate the lore of various kinds of Eastern mystical teachers. They all recounted to him tales of the miracles and the sayings of the founders and great teachers of their schools, all long dead.

When he returned home, he submitted his report, which contained the single word "Carrots."

He was called upon to explain himself. Nasrudin told the King: "The best part is buried; few know—except the farmer—by the green that there is orange underground; if you don't work for it, it will deteriorate; there are a great many donkeys associated with it."

—From *The Exploits of the Incomparable Mulla Nasrudin*[1]

The Hindus have recognized for centuries four *yogas** or paths of self-development of comparable rank, each one most

---

* *Yoga* derives from *yuj*, to yoke. This root has an implication of union and also of discipline. The word might be rendered, therefore, as a yoking one's self to a discipline conducive to union, or as a discipline in union (to the self, in most formulations of yoga) which is both a path and, when perfected, the goal. Cf. the etymology of *religion* according to Christian authors: re-ligion, to re-unite.

suited to a particular type of individual and a possible path to the common goal of all paths and all men: karma yoga, or the way of action; bhakti yoga, the way of love; gnani yoga, the way of knowledge; and raja yoga (literally the "royal yoga") which has elements of the other three but is characterized by techniques of mind control and meditation.*

The will, the feelings, and the cognitive processes have represented a threefold distinction in psychology since Brentano's day, and these three, as well as consciousness, have been seen as the ideals of human development in the West as in the East. Even beyond the explicit recognition of a given approach as pertaining to the domain of action, feeling, knowing, or awareness, I think that these categories—stemming from our psychological structure—are useful as a classification scheme that may apply beyond cultural frontiers.

Accordingly, I have chosen to apply this scheme throughout the pages which follow and thus I am inviting the reader to group the multiplicity of the ways of growth into the four categories of action, feeling, knowing, and awareness, a grouping marked by similarities in techniques and intent.

This intent though, it must be added, is not always retained by those who repeat mechanically the old formulas; actions which were instruments of "fire-making" † have all too often become objects of worship on their own; the feelings that are a natural response to fire have been turned into devotion to particular individuals in the past; and the knowledge that is meant to be lived has become a substitute for life in myth,

---

* Hatha yoga, consisting in physical exercises, is not considered to be an independent path, but an adjunct to other yogas—mainly to meditation. Nadi or chakra yoga and kundalini yoga may be regarded as specialized forms of raja yoga, or the advanced aspect of hatha yoga if the term is used to designate more than the purely physical aspect of the discipline.

† See pp. 46 ff.

faith, or intellectualism. Precisely in view of this alienation of forms and techniques from their source in meaning, I have emphasized the purport of the ways rather than their technical details, which may be readily found in other sources.

In each of the following sections I am speaking of *ways* rather than of a single way of action, feeling, knowing, and awareness. This refers not only to the cultural and descriptive diversity of forms in which a given approach is embodied but also to the fact that, when we look at the techniques in a historical perspective, we can also find broad differences in strategy within at least each of the four major groups.

The Ways of Action

From times immemorial men seem to have been concerned with the idea that action is not only relevant to the attainment of external and practical aims—the consequences of action—but also to the question of self-cultivation and self-realization. Moreover, man's question as to what to do to attain spiritual fulfillment has been answered by religious and mystical traditions in a fashion that considers no single action of a person as irrelevant to such a goal. Speaking of karma yoga, the yoga of action, Haridas Chaudhuri describes what can be applied to every integral discipline of the spirit, for each discipline entails action as an element or component:

> The yoga of action lays stress upon the volitional side of human nature. It regards the will to live, the striving for growth and perfection, as the natural starting point for spiritual training. Action is indeed of the very essence of life. No man can ever stop acting. The question is whether he is engaged in some fruitful action or in meaningless action. The inescapable need for action is reflected in the popular saying: "An idle man's brain is the devil's workshop."
> When a person withdraws from the outside world and shuts

himself up in his solitary room, he is still acting. His action may assume the form of uncontrolled day-dreaming or free floating on the clouds of fancy. Or, it may assume the form of detached contemplation of past experiences or methodical self-inquiry. Or, he may find himself with an empty mind ringing with the jarring voices of unwelcome guests from the tombs of the unconscious. Even when a person goes to the hills, he may carry the whole of society upon his shoulders. His unfulfilled desires and repressed wishes are sure to accompany him everywhere. He withdraws from all purposive action only to find his mental vacuum filled with the ineffectual self-paintings of the repressed libido.

So the yoga of action seeks to solve the basic problem of man on the basis of properly guided action. It is particularly suitable for those who are men of active habits. It tries to regulate one's life of action in such a way that spiritual freedom and self-fulfillment can be attained through a re-fashioning of the whole business of living.[2]

Chaudhuri then examines what "spiritual action" is, and concludes that it means "selfless dedication to human welfare on the basis of one's free self-development. . . . To be true to one's own self" is the first prerequisite of social service. That is the only way of offering one's best to society. The first and foremost duty of every individual is to develop his latent possibilities.

RIGHT ACTION

One of the ways in which daily activity can be seen as spiritually relevant may be summarized in the notion of *right action*. In Buddhism, right action is that which proceeds from *dharma* (from the root *dhr,* to sustain). In Taoism right action or virtue (*Tê*) is conduct in accordance with Tao, the way. Thus according to Taoism, each thing in the universe has its

Tao. There is the Tao of heaven and that of the earth; and as every tree has its own Tao, man has too; every individual may or may not be in accordance with his Way, the way of his own nature. In the theistic language of the Judaeo-Christian tradition, Tao, the will of the cosmos, is expressed as God's will.

It is perhaps a temptation of our modern minds (seeking the specific means whereby of everything) to think of psychological exercises as something outside the context of life, and perhaps conceive of them as a substitute for life or at least as a "self-realization" compartment set aside from the compartment of practicality and everyday affairs. It may be well to bear in mind that the great spiritual systems throughout history did not conceive of such a boundary.

In Patanjali's yoga, for instance, the practice of meditation (*dharana*, *dhyana*, and *samadhi*) that crowns the system is seen as inseparable from, and its successful practice possible only if accompanied by the observance in everyday life of *yama* and *niyama*, constraint and discipline. The content of self-restraint and of the specific observances in Patanjali's time and place may be different from what would be most effective or desirable in our midst, but the point here is that the effort involved in such constraint and discipline is not substantially different from that involved in the more subtle exercises of meditation. *Yama* and *niyama* are preparatory limbs of yoga in that they embody—in the most concrete and visible way—principles such as detachment and self-control which will later become a more direct object of the practice. From *yama* and *niyama* relevant to behavior, the disciple will pass on to postures, breath control, and only then to the purely psychological exercises. On the other hand, as Professor Spiegelberg remarks:

> It is taken for granted that anyone who enters on the path of yoga can be able to bear at least sufficient self-control not to be utterly

at the mercy of every mood and caprice, nor to surrender at once to every sensual impulse. Beyond this, concentration and self-knowledge are necessary as foundations for any ascension to a higher plane; and moral purity must come before everything else, since a burdened conscience and feelings of remorse are the greatest conceivable obstacles on the path that is to be followed.[3]

Buddhism has a similar approach to meditation, which is not regarded as an isolated practice but part of a system, the first stage of which is the observance of the precepts. Furthermore, the precepts would in turn be of limited significance if seen as purely behavioral observances. Their deeper aim is to facilitate the emergence of an attitude or realization identical to the goal of meditation, and to stabilize this attainment in the midst of life: "To laugh without leaving behind any trace of the laughter," writes Abbot Obora of the Soto Zen sect, "to weep without leaving any trace of the tears, to rejoice without anything of that rejoicing remaining behind—this is a state of lightness, and to be able to live in it is the life of Emptiness, life with nothing at its heart." [4]

What right action or God's will is for a given individual at a given time is for him to find out with the totality of his faculties.* Yet it is conceivable that certain generalities may be regarded as the most probable channels of right action in a given culture and in a given set of circumstances. This is the basis of the Judaic conception of God's Law. While in its detail the Law consisted for its greater part of "statutes relating to different sections of the community and to its multifarious institutions, ecclesiastical as well as civil"—statutes that had been

---

* This is also a matter in which the role of the spiritual guide of many traditions is of great importance. The guide, having found his own place in the cosmos, may help another to find his.

obsolete for centuries*—such institutions were, at that time, part of the kingdom of God.

> And here lay the strength of Judaism. The modern man is an eclectic being. He takes his religion from the Bible, his laws from the Romans, his culture from the classics, and his politics from his party. He is certainly broader in his sympathies than the Jew of old; but as a composite being, he must necessarily be lacking in harmony and unity. His sympathies are divided between the different sources of his inspiration—sources which do not, as we know, always go well together. In order to avoid collision, he has at last to draw the line between the ecclesiastical and the civil, leaving the former, which in fact was forced upon him by a foreign religious conqueror, to a separate body of men whose business it is to look after the welfare of his invisible soul, whilst reserving the charge of the body and the world to himself.

> The Rabbinic notion seems to have been that "if religion is anything, it is everything." [6]

Schechter comments that the old Rabbinic literature is even devoid of the words *spiritual* and *material,* the "things of heaven" covering a much wider area of human life than is commonly imagined. And he relates that when Hillel the Great (the inspirer of the saying "Let all thy deeds be for the sake of Heaven") was about to take a bath, he said "I am going to perform a religious act by beautifying my person, that was created in the image of God."

Understandably, principles that were once observed as means to man's inner unfolding became ends themselves—moral injunctions based on no more than authority and custom. So much so that we are prone to see social convenience only at the root of the commandments of different cultures, and we distrust the idea of duty as being a matter of superego

---

* "The laws . . . relating to idolatry, incest, and the sacrifices of children to Moloch, could hardly be considered as coming within the province of the practical life even of the pre-Christian Jew." [5]

commands resulting from the internalization of parental or societal norms. However true it is that this is the psychological
nature of duty in most individuals, a one-sided view of right
action may blind us today to the significance of everyday life
as a *way,* just as it did in the times of the Sermon on the Mount
or the *Dhammapada.* Or, as Basho stated it: "Do not follow in
the footsteps of the ancients, seek what they sought."

Right action as a way is not "right" in a moral sense, but in
that of being conducive to man's development. It may do this
by guiding him into doing what "his nature" really wants to
do. Precisely in discussing the Jewish law, which is so remarkable for its quality of command, Schechter comments "that the
whole man stands in the service of God, each limb or member
of his body being entrusted with the execution of its respective
functions." The injunction "seek the Lord and live," therefore,
can be interpreted as "be yourself."

The general trend in both psychotherapy and education
today is away from ready-made answers, models, and even advice. This is an understandable reaction to a stifling misuse of
fixed forms that has been part of our culture for centuries. A
deteriorated version of the principle of right action, in fact,
after a while tends to operate spontaneously aside from deliberate prescriptions of behavior. A certain type of psychological
refinement and subtlety is manifested in certain gestures, for
instance. The gestures reveal the quality from which they proceed, and persons with a yearning for that quality may seek to
incorporate these external forms. Finally, these become the
mannerisms conventionally regarded as elegant, and the lack
of them is regarded as vulgar. A king of England, moved by
Handel's *Messiah,* breaks conventional formalism by standing
up during the performance. During the following years, when
the noblemen stand up at the sound of the Hallelujah chorus,

they are awakened to the music by their own gesture and the memory of their king's action. Later, though, this becomes an empty ritual; a must, divorced from the feeling in which it originated and which the gesture could serve to recapture.

In a culture in which people have been enacting shallow rituals like these for too long, the first task of psychotherapy is that of liberating the individual from that dead and deadening weight, and making him receptive to what Maslow calls the "inner voices."

Still, in even the most "client-centered" instances of successful psychotherapy we can see the individual gradually readjusting his life situation, until a pattern emerges which he feels is "right." He then feels happy, and we may wonder if his well-being is the *source* of his newly acquired freedom to rule his own life or if it is instead the *consequence* of a life which is in harmony with the law of his being, of a life which his new freedom has made possible. From this point of view, practically all forms of psychotherapy may be seen as ways of liberating the individual to his own identity and vocation. Therapies are to the inner calling like a path leading to a greater path.

Aside from this function of freeing the individual (through understanding of his hindrances and support of authenticity and risk), the therapies may also constitute a more or less conscious search for the individual's right action, but the way in which the matter is approached is the opposite of that of the Law or the Precepts.

THE WAY OF ATTUNEMENT OR SELF-OBEDIENCE

Just as the direction of personal development can be either ready-made or found anew in every instance, in the matter of action, too, we find two opposite approaches that lead to the same goal. One is that of precepts and discipline, ideals and duty, injunctions and restraint; it is a way of friction, wherein the individual can grow to know his imperfections and develop his will. The other is a way of self-trust and self-expression, not constrained by the enacting of ideals. In this view, freedom itself should lead to growing beyond wrong action or imperfection, by providing the greatest occasion for experience and choice. By following his desires the individual will learn to discern those that stem from his real needs and those which originate in his past conditioning and only lead him to dead ends and mirages. He will thus become *attuned* to his real structure, function, and style. In this way he will find God's will "from the Spirit" rather than from the Law as embodied in parents, church, or injunctions of his culture. This approach is not exclusively the attitude of contemporary therapies. It is found in such ancient ways as Taoism or tantric yoga, in every flexible form of education, and it is to some extent the way of every human being who implicitly trusts his preferences. Tantric yoga, though, epitomizes such an approach and for this reason it holds special significance to anybody interested in the ways. Chaudhuri writes:

> *Tantric* yoga is boldly affirmative in its methodological approach. Other yoga systems have laid much stress upon renunciation and desirelessness as essential aids to liberation. But *Tantric* yoga affirms the need for intelligent and organized fulfilment of natural desires. In its view there is no basic antagonism between nature and spirit. Nature is the creative power of spirit in the objective sphere. Nobody therefore can enter the kingdom of spirit without first obtaining a passport from nature. Practice of austerity, asceticism and self-mortification is an insult to nature. It creates more difficulties than it can solve. By weakening the body and producing inner conflicts and tensions, it undermines balanced and

healthy development. It is only by following the spirit of nature that one can swim with the current and capture the kingdom of heaven by storm.

Worship of the Divine Mother implies appreciation of the presence of profound wisdom in nature, both external and internal. There is a principle of cosmic intelligence operative in external nature. It controls the process of cosmic evolution. Similarly, there is deep wisdom inherent in man's inner nature, in his unconscious psyche. It secretly determines his inner evolution. If a person intelligently follows the bent of his own nature, his desires become more and more refined and lofty. Base desires gradually yield place to noble desires. Lower impulses are replaced by higher impulses. When a child's natural desire to play with toys is duly satisfied, it is soon outgrown, yielding place to a keen interest in books or living playmates. When a man's natural desire for sex is lawfully satisfied, it gives rise to a growing interest in social welfare or humanitarian service. When his desire for enjoying the world is duly satisfied on the basis of intelligent self-organization, one day it gives rise to a deeper longing for Transcendence.

So *Tantric* yoga prescribes what is called desireful prayer and worship (*sakama upasana*). All natural desires are accepted as modes of manifestation of the creative spirit of nature. The problem is to organize them intelligently with a view to the maximum satisfaction and fulfilment of one's nature. There is divine sanction behind such self-fulfilment. One places one's desires before God, and then, with God's sanction and sanctification, proceeds to fulfill them in a spirit of self-offering to the Divine. This brings about an increasing refinement and spiritual transformation of one's desire-nature. A constructive channelling of the libido towards the higher ends of existence takes place.[7]

Though each one of the ways might be examined from the point of view of action, some operate most specifically in this domain, and are more appropriate illustrations of the process of achieving self-knowledge through self-expression. I will briefly comment upon some:

(1) Deconditioning techniques are used in behavior therapy (Wolpe's "reciprocal inhibition")[8] and in Russian applications of reflexology.[9] What is obtained by these techniques is the extinction of self-limiting responses. Although this is not part of the formulations of behavior therapy, we have reason to assume that the old ("inappropriate") response is not replaced by a new conditioned response, but merely extinguished, and thus the individual is made free to choose; he is now ready to respond with his organismic preferences to the demands of reality. An implicit fear-arousing presupposition has been cleared away through contact with an avoided aspect of reality and, at least in this restricted area of experience, "truth has set him free."

(2) What behavior therapy does in connection with very restricted and particular conditionings, theater games and role-playing techniques do with regard to the broad conditioned patterns of response that we call character structures. In forcing himself to act in a style unlike "his own"—even in the context of the "as if" situation of therapy or play—the individual characteristically discovers that his habitual pattern is compulsive and rigid. In playing his most incompatible roles he attains a new freedom of response, a new expressive repertoire that may facilitate an inner freedom of experiencing, and he has occasion to be more aware of the fears that constrain him. In these methods, as in deconditioning techniques, the individual is not exactly learning to attune himself to his pattern of right action, but is attaining the freedom to act upon preferences or reason—a precondition for attunement. Not driven by compulsion, he may now be able to base his actions and reactions upon another source.

The two types of techniques commented upon above are ways of breaking the rigidity of ordinary personality, and allowing the pseudospontaneity of what is habitual to give way to the real spontaneity of self-expression. In this they may be compared to the discipline of obedience to a rule in monastic communities and obedience to a teacher in spiritual guidance. An important function of the latter is found in the perceptive-behavior therapist who can push the individual into confronting what he avoids and developing what in his avoidance he has failed to develop.

I think these considerations may be valuable to hold in mind when we reflect upon the place of obedience and discipline in the education of the young. Instead of a discipline that stifles and kills spontaneity, can we not think of a discipline (and even obedience) that "un-limits" the individual, which pushes him over his own limitations? How can we avoid the danger of making obedience a means of conditioning and, instead, use it to liberate the child from conditioned fears?

(3) The basic-encounter group is, to a considerable extent, an exercise in risk-taking, spontaneity, and authenticity in a social setting. In learning-theory terms, we might say that authenticity is rewarded—until it may become its own reward. It is an occasion for the relinquishing of obsolete responses and an experiment in freedom in which the individual may find his own style and form—hitherto buried under his defense mechanisms and roles.

(4) The question of attunement is tackled quite directly by sensory awareness at the most elemental level of physical functioning. In ways which in writing would seem too simple to be of any consequence, a capable teacher here comes back again and again to the question of how we permit or we interfere with the elemental functions of standing, lying, walking, breathing, and so on. Are we really standing the way we want to stand? Are our shoulders where *they* want to be? How are we distributing the weight of our body between our legs? Are our knees locked or slightly bent? And is the way in which we hold

them the one that gives us maximum comfort? Is our abdomen held in or protruding? And how does it feel to have it either way? Does it affect breathing in any way? And, above all else, do we have a preference? In this way we learn to become receptive to our organismic needs and let go of extrinsically determined habits or unnecessary tensions. We become attuned to the requirements of our mechanism, and learn to disregard both the so-called right postures introjected from fashion and the wrong postures that derive from lack of awareness of our concrete reality.

In the process of becoming attuned—through the practice of attention—to such simple aspects of our activity as the most functional way to bounce a ball or sit, the practice of sensory awareness contributes, I believe, to the development of an attitude of far wider applicability: a receptivity to the reality of a situation and of our needs, and a detachment from automatic responses. This may explain why peak-experiences occur quite frequently in practice meetings.

(5) The kind of psychotherapy that is carried out in the altered states of consciousness elicited by drugs may be seen also in the light of the principle outlined in these pages as a technique that develops a receptivity toward promptings deeper than those of habitual behavior in order to find from within the pattern of right action that social conditioning had been obscuring. That the hallucinogens interfere with conditioning is clear enough from experiments with animals, but the positive consequence of this is not generally made explicit: the possibility of new responses toward the environment during the period in which the learned patterns have fallen into temporary abeyance. In these states the individual is, in a way, stripped of his personality and afforded an opportunity to contemplate his essence.

(6) An experimentation in freedom and a practice in surren-

der to spontaneous promptings deeper than those of learned roles is also involved in the sessions of Subud groups.[10] What is redundantly called the practice of the *latihan*,* in fact, elicits different types of experience that resemble closely those brought about by psychedelic drugs. Subud is an exercise in attunement *par excellence* or, at least, by definition—for it purports to be an act of surrender to God's will as perceived (non-conceptually) at the moment, from within, rather than accepted from without in the shape of norm or ritual.

(7) Along with the above-listed approaches we should mention a number of informal approaches to art education which constitute an important trend in our day. In these the materials of art—paints, movements, sounds—are taken as a medium for the exploration of the individual's spontaneity, through which he may gradually discover his unique preferences, his individual expression, his style. Of course, this has been achieved by every true artist, but the traditional emphasis in the artist's development has been less improvisational and more intent upon the imitation of fixed, ideal forms. Valuable as that traditional attitude may be in principle, it can only fulfill its purpose when accompanied by an understanding of how to *use* this discipline of imitation and these forms. This understanding—an example of that which makes authority a liberating rather than a limiting force—seems to survive in Eastern cultures† but has been long absent in ours. Consequently, geniuses have only rarely emerged from schools of fine arts, and artists who understand what they are doing are critical of the imposition of value judgments that is still prevalent in schools for children and artists.

* The Indonesian word *latihan*, now an international term, literally means "practice" or "exercise."

† Mrs. Herrigel's account of her experiences while learning *ikebana* in Japan[11] and Mr. Herrigel's discussion of archery[12] express the point well.

In contrast to the conventional approach to art education there is a growing tendency among teachers to teach techniques only, and thus provide the potential artist with the opportunity of expressing himself. Some of these art teachers, guided by their intuitive understanding, have been able to bring about in their students a process of contact with and insight into themselves which transcends the conventional goal of the artistic endeavor. Because of this, a number of them have become more interested in the use of artistic activity for the purpose of self-development rather than for the artistic work itself.

 THE WAY OF RIGHT DOING: ACTION THAT IS NONACTION

The relevance of action to the spiritual quest is not only in terms of *what* is being done, or right action proper, but of *how* it is done—right doing, whatever the action in hand. This approach has been cultivated as a way in different schools, but is a most prominent feature in the dervish tradition and in Zen Buddhism, where it has created cultural forms like the Japanese art of archery and the tea ceremony. Gurdjieff, who had a dervish background, is reported to have said: "If you can serve a cup of tea right, you can do *anything*."

A living example of right doing (which also shows some of the grounds and implications of Gurdjieff's statement) may be found in anecdotes of Rikkyu, the originator of the Japanese tea ceremony. It is said that Rikkyu's powerful patron once invited a well-known general to this ceremony, and the latter was struck by Rikkyu's precise and economical movements. From his specialized point of view, he noticed that Rikkyu never presented an opening for a possible attack, and his vanity was touched enough that he decided to strike the master lightly with his fan as soon as this were possible. Near the end of the ceremony, when the general thought that at last he had seen an opening, Rikkyu looked up at him with a smile, and complimented his patron for having such a fine warrior in his retinue.[13]

This story shows that the common quality required by the tea ceremony and the military art consists of a certain state of mind, of which attentiveness is a foremost attitude. Right doing involves more than mechanical adequacy in the action being undertaken. This is the outward aspect of what is being sought by the doer; the inner aspects are the proper attitude and proper relationship to the action. "Proper" here, like "right," does not refer to normative criteria, but to something that is dictated by a profound, rather than superficial, reality. Attention is only one of its characteristics. For instance, one of the principles in karma yoga is that of detachment from the fruits of action, so that whatever is done is done for its own sake. This principle, again, is not a moralistic one but stems from the experience of man in a certain self-validating state of consciousness, where such detachment not only is natural, but originates in a *realization* of independence from the stream of events, and is the outcome of a shift in world view. By acting *as if* he were in such a state of mind a person might expect to facilitate the emergence of it as a reality, just as an actor may facilitate with his words and actions the emergence of the feelings and views of his character. (Feelings that are not imaginary, for he would not be able to summon them up if they were not part of him anyway.)

Attention and detachment—the two attitudes mentioned above—might seem to be quite unrelated states of mind, but are in fact only conceptually independent from one another. Still another anecdote from the life of a Japanese tea master can serve to convey a sense of their meeting ground.

The tea master was challenged to a duel by an unscrupulous *ronin** who was trying to scare the tea man and extort money from him. There being no way to decline with honor, the tea man resolved that he would die well.

He visited a neighboring fencing teacher and requested that the swordsman teach him the art of dying. "You have a unique request," the teacher replied. "I will be happy to grant your wish, but first, please serve me a cup of tea." The tea man was only too glad to make tea for the fencing master, because this was most likely his last chance to practice his art. Forgetting all about the duel, the tea master serenely proceeded to prepare tea, as if this were all that seriously concerned him at the moment.

The swordsman was deeply impressed with his concentrated state of mind, from which all the superficial stirrings of consciousness were swept away. He exclaimed, "There you are! No need for you to learn the art of death. Your present state of mind is enough for you to cope with any swordsman. When you see your *ronin*, do this: First, think you are going to serve tea for a guest. Courteously salute him, apologizing for the delay and tell him that you are now ready for the contest. Take off your outer coat, fold it up carefully, and then put your fan on it, just as you do when you are at work. Draw your sword, lift it high over your head, in full readiness to strike down the opponent, and collect your thoughts for a combat. When he attacks, strike him with your sword. It will probably end in a mutual slaying." The tea man thanked the sword-master for his instruction and went back to the place where he had promised to meet his opponent.

He scrupulously followed the swordsman's advice with the same attitude of mind as when he was serving tea for his friends. When, boldly standing before the *ronin*, he raised his sword, the *ronin* saw an altogether different personality before him. He saw no opening, for the tea man now appeared to him as an embodiment of fearlessness. And throwing up his sword, he prostrated himself on the ground and asked the tea man's pardon for his rude behavior.[14]

Right doing, as this narration illustrates, is a discipline of

* A wandering Samurai.

meditation in action, and at least as complex as meditation itself. It is a practice in awareness, in detachment from self-interest, in wholeheartedness, in openness to reality, in being available to the task at hand, in unification of body, feelings, and thought, and in many other qualities insofar as we choose to regard them as different from one another.*

Anything said on the subject of action in general may be applied to those kinds of action that are devoid of practicality and exist only as a way—or for themselves. This is the case of ritual, and that of art. Art might be conceived of as a condensation of life, and life as an extended work of art that we can create day after day. For the artist right doing is his being himself to the fullest in his act of creation; right doing, beyond technical perfection, amounts to his being his best self at the moment, for the perfect act is inseparable from the perfect state of mind. The practical implications of life pull us in different directions and stand in conflict with our performing our everyday actions for ourselves—that is, for our disinterested aim, paradoxical as this may sound. Art and ritual, by contrast, are *only* for ourselves, or for themselves, so that we can find ourselves in being for them, in enacting them. They are occasions for the experience of that perfect attitude that can then be taken into everyday life.

Seen from the point of view of right doing our culture is poor, both in its daily expression and in the domain of specialized techniques. The so-called materialism of the Western world is a theoretical stance: in fact, it is a denial of the appreciation of matter. As Alan Watts has remarked:

> For surely a materialist is a person who loves material—wood and
> leather, flax and silk, eggs and fruit, stone and glass, fish and

* For a discussion of the experiential oneness of conceptually distinct processes entailed by the ways, see Chapter IV.

bread, olives and wine. Yet, almost without exception, every American town and village looks as if it were made by people who loathed material and wanted to convert it as fast as possible into heaps of rubbish. . . . The kitchens look like operating rooms and everything that comes out of them tastes as if it had been washed in soap, and made by chemists instead of cooks . . .

All jesting aside, however, I would point to such cooking as the main sign that American culture is not only post-Christian but anti-Christian. Proper cooking can be done only in the spirit of a sacrament and a ritual. It is an act of worship and thanksgiving, a celebration of the glory of life, and no one can cook well who does not love and respect the raw materials he handles: the eggs and onions, the herbs and salts, the mushrooms and beans, and, above all, the living animals—fish, fowl, and flesh—whose lives we take to live. Ritual is not just a symbolism of formal gestures. Ritual is, basically, anything done with loving awareness and reverence— whether cooking, carpentry, fishing, writing a letter, performing surgery, or making love. The everyday life of the modern West is quite startlingly lacking in ritual, as in all the style and color that goes with it.[15]

If the Christian spirit is in the hallowing of bread and wine, "Christianity" with its disregard of the senses is distinctly anti-Christian.

Our disregard for the perfection and enjoyment of forms is part of our greedy utilitarianism, our concern with quantity, our future orientation, and our competitiveness. In contrast with our concern for external effectiveness and perfection of form, Orientals in general seem to have retained, more than we have, the notion of action as an occasion for a perfect attitude and internal effectiveness. I have been told that not long ago the members of a team of American baseball players, visiting Japan for a contest, were surprised to see how the Japanese kept their bats in individual bags, almost like holy objects, and accused themselves of not practicing "seriously" enough. Obviously, the perfection they were striving for was not merely that of measurable success. It was the same kind of perfection that the teacher of archery requires when he criticizes a student after an accurate shot. Not understanding that the target is not the target, more than one Western student has felt perplexed or hurt in his pride at such criticism.

The kinds of action devoid of practicality that we are discussing—art and ritual—require more than any other way, in order to be right doing, a teacher who embodies and conveys nonverbally the attitude at the heart of his specific discipline. Aside from the case of sensory awareness (which belongs here as much as in the discussion on attunement), we do not have schools or traditions purporting to do anything comparable to the Eastern arts. This, to be sure, is done to a greater or lesser extent by individual teachers in the arts, crafts, and even sports, but their attainments have not developed to the extent of a self-conscious formulation and a reliable transmission. However, the recognition of nonutilitarian and intrinsic values in the sphere of movement is evidenced by the development of refined forms of movement therapy and in the growing interest in dance as a discipline divorced from performance. Mention should also be made here of the new approach to massage cultivated at Esalen Institute, which, in its best expression, may be rightly regarded as an art and a form of meditation in action.*

I believe that our culture, torn between a disembodied life of the spirit and a value-deprived practicality, has more to learn from the Orient in this particular sphere of *practical spirituality* than any other. Perhaps the growing interest in *tai chi*

* Once more, given its purely attitudinal and inward nature, this practice has not yet found a translator into the medium of the written word. B. Gunther's booklet *Getting in Touch with Massage*[16] is suggestive.

chuan,[17] in Japanese techniques of self-defense, in calligraphy, and in other disciplines cultivated in the Orient, as well as the activity of Sufi circles, may serve as a basis for the development of ways reflecting our own style.

The Ways of Feeling

Action is the outer part of man, and whenever it is a matter of choice rather than automatic habit it expresses an inner world of feelings. Hence the word *e-motion:* it *moves* us. The ways of action attempt to reach the inner through the outer. Man can know himself, express, and realize himself through his actions, and thus develop. But there are ways which focus more directly on feelings than others.

As with action, we may conceive of right feelings and wrong feelings, not in terms of any authoritarian or extrinsic value but in terms of reality at the moment and the function of an organism. Such a notion of right and wrong is implicit when we speak of "emotional disturbances," the target of psychiatry. And just as we posited that right action is not that which follows an external dictate but one which is in accordance with the Tao, with the deeper laws of the organism, so we can conceive that right feelings are those always present in us which constitute our *real* feelings, but which are covered up by the reactive feelings that take so much of our conscious attention. If this concept is accepted we can see how a change in feelings (transformation, psychological healing) relates to the *development* of feelings: as real feelings develop, they tend to sweep aside the less real feelings that constitute affective disturbances, the pseudofeelings that veil the genuine ones. That the "negative" feelings constituting neurotic reactions are less real than others does not appear to be subjectively true, but it is psychologically defensible on the grounds that they do not

stem from the real self but from an idealized self that is ultimately a fiction, a product of the imagination, and that they
are not responses to a real situation but to an interpretation of
reality in terms of childish fantasies.

Even if we do not want to go so far as to speak of a relative
unreality of neurotic feelings, we may still accept the notion of
two sets of feelings: those of the real self in us, and those of the
constructs we house in our psyche—identifications, social roles,
and a proud self-ideal. How can the former be developed and
the latter minimized?

Robert De Ropp, in the chapter of his book *The Master Game*
that deals with the education of emotions, says:

> Whitman, it appears, was equipped with an emotional brain so
> harmonized and balanced that it simply did not generate those
> poisons which spoil the lives of others not so gifted. One might jus-
> tifiably call him a "natural saint." The question is whether, by
> any means at all, the emotional brain of one less gifted can be
> trained to function in a similar way. Following Paul of Tarsus, we
> may accept the idea that love is the highest of all positive emo-
> tions and admit that we are merely sounding brass without it even
> though we do speak with the tongues of men and of angels. But
> can a man learn to love? Can the emotional center be educated to
> generate this high emotion? Can this function (the genesis of love)
> ever be brought under the control of the conscious will?
>
> Obviously the founder of Christianity thought that it could. "A
> new commandment give I you, that ye love one another." Would
> he have given such a command if its fulfillment had been physi-
> cally impossible?
>
> Alas, the history of the Christian Church gives us little reassur-
> ance. We read of crusades, massacres, burnings, torturings, a hide-
> ous catalog of cruelty compiled by Inquisitors and fanatics. These
> "servants of the God of Love" not only failed to learn to love each
> other, but also used their religion as an excuse for hating and per-
> formed, in the name of the loving Savior, actions that would have

made a Yahoo blush. If the cruelty of man has become less in recent times, it is certainly not on account of the influence of the
Christian Church.

Love, hope and faith are not emotions that can be learned. This is the
conclusion to which we are forced by all the evidence available. It
is easy to teach men to hate. The efficacy of wartime propaganda
makes this clear. It may be possible, though not easy, to teach
them not to hate, to recognize hatred as an evil emotion, one not
worthy of civilized beings. But to teach them positively to love in
an objective, universal way is not possible.[18]

Such a pessimistic conclusion, though, stems from the contemplation of historical events rather than from the results attained by serious followers of the Way of Love for the purpose
of self-perfection. One might object to De Ropp's conclusions
in the same terms in which Herbert Fingarette[19] objects to
Freud's criticism of religion: just as Freud analyzed a popular
sentiment rather than instances of religious experience, De
Ropp contemplates the deplorable condition of the masses
rather than the evolution of the few who have chosen the disciplines of feeling-transformation—theistic mysticism, bhakti
yoga, or present-day psychotherapies.

In the domain of feelings, as in that of action, we can contrast the approach of pursuing an ideal by moving against the
tendencies of the moment—that is, by disciplining imperfections—with that which pursues that ideal by reflecting the
tendencies of the moment in all their imperfections. In the
former the aim is to cultivate the most real and basic feelings,
which are assumed to be those of love toward all beings and a
sense of sacredness in all things, and to uproot the negative
feelings by denying them attention and expression. In the latter, the way is that of catharsis, by which the person gets rid of
his psychological debris by giving them expression. The former
has traditionally been the way of the monk, and the latter is

that of the patient in most forms of psychological treatment. Prayer and detachment from or suppression of "wrong" feelings are typical of the first approach, while honest communication, whether in confession, friendship, or on the analytical couch, are typical of the second. Art lies between the two, in that it can be approached as a way to express either the inner or the outer, the truth or its distortions, ideal beauty or the neurotic state of the moment. Great art and different forms of worship or cult-experience are an embodiment of man's unfulfilled and unexpressed deeper reality. They may be regarded as vessels of collective expression, with whose forms man can identify and establish indirect contact with himself.

DEVOTIONALISM

The mysticism of love and union responds, according to Happold, to an urge

. . . to escape from a sense of separation, from the loneliness of selfhood, towards a closer participation and reunion with Nature and God, which will bring peace and rest to the soul. . . .

This urge has its origin, if one accepts the only thesis on which a case for the validity of mysticism is based, in the fact that man is in some way a sharer in the divine life. He therefore longs to return to that from which he feels he has come, to be more closely and consciously linked with it. He feels himself to be a pilgrim of eternity, a creature in time but a citizen of a timeless world.

Since man is a sharer in the divine life, there is a mutual and reciprocal attraction. The mysticism of love and union can be described not only in terms of man's search for God but also in terms of God's search for man.

"I sought for God for thirty years," writes the Moslem mystic Abu Yazid. "I thought it was I who desired Him, but, no, it was He who desired me." [20]

To say that devotional mysticism springs from an urge to transcend the limits of individuality and attain union with God amounts to saying that the love of God is motivated by the love of God. But there is a further claim in mysticism: that the feeling of love for God is a pathway to the experience of mystical union. As the unknown author of *The Cloud of Unknowing* states:

> For of all other creatures and their works, yea, and of the works of God's self, may a man through grace have fullhead of knowing, and well he can think of them: but of God Himself can no man think. And therefore I would leave all that thing that I can think, and choose to my love that thing that I cannot think. For why; He may well be loved, but not thought. By love may He be gotten and holden; but by thought never.[21]

In terms of the Freudian notion of sublimation of libidinal impulses, mysticism could be regarded as a flight from reality, a substitution of "God" for the immediate objects of desire and a form of wish fulfillment in fantasy and symbol rather than actuality. The mystic's view is just the opposite: he regards the many earthly desires of common man as substitutes for what he really wants, a groping in all directions for waters that do not quench his thirst. All our desires originate, whether we know it or not, from a longing for God, and we go after different objects on the assumption that in them we will find what we seek. The mystic's path is, therefore, one of a refinement of love in which he outgrows worldly vanities and, like a growing boy that loses interest in his childish toys, he directs his attention to the essential:

> The yoga of love starts with the natural feelings and emotions of the human heart. Love of the self, the desire to serve the beloved, love of playmates, affection for parents and children, the love of the spouse, are the most fundamental modes of human emotion.

The technique of the yoga of love consists in turning them more and more to God, the ultimate ground of existence. An increasing spiritual orientation of natural emotions is the secret here.

Love of one's own self is the most elemental emotion in man. The instinct of self-preservation, the search for liberty, security and happiness, the longing for recognition and renown, are the different forms of manifestation of elemental self-love. The yoga of love shows how through a proper tutoring and deepening of one's basic sense of self-interest, the energy of self-love can be directed to the Divine. The Divine is not only the creator and loving preserver of all existence. The Divine is also one's true inmost Self, the all-controlling higher Self. The orientation of self-love to God is called *Santa*.

The spirit of service (*seva*) is an essential component of love. Rooted in the heart of every man is a strong desire to render loving service to the benefactor, to the well-wisher, to the protector and provider. Sacrifices are gladly made to please him. The yoga of love seeks to turn this spirit of service and self-sacrifice to God who is the ultimate protector and provider for all living creatures. This is the usual pattern in all popular religions. A pious man takes refuge in God as the sovereign master and ruler of the universe. He looks upon himself as a humble servant of God, the supreme Lord of the world. He experiences perfect security and happiness in the service of the Divine. This is called *Dasya*.

Then there is the natural longing for companionship and friendship. This longing can be turned to God. God may be regarded as man's unfailing friend and ever-present companion. Even in his absolute loneliness, he need not be afraid nor feel helpless. Even when the whole world deserts him, he may count upon God as his eternal friend, philosopher and guide. Such a spiritual orientation of the need for friendship is called *Sakhya*.

Then there is the sweet love-relationship between parent and child. Such a love-relationship can easily be established between man and the supreme ruling power of the universe. The cosmic ruler may be regarded as the heavenly Father or the heavenly

Mother, according to the strongest emotional need of the individual. In doing so one's devotion to father or mother is religiously sublimated. It brings happiness, peace and security to the individual and makes his life profoundly meaningful. In a matriarchal society it is natural to conceive of God as the cosmic Mother. In a patriarchal society it is natural to think of God as the heavenly Father. In a country like India where matriarchal and patriarchal societies have flourished for long side by side, mutually influencing each other, the cosmic principle comes to be regarded as the heavenly Father-Mother, with an equal accent upon both aspects. So the Divine in Hindu philosophy is Siva-Sakti, Iswara-Maya, Radha-Krsna, Ram-Sita, etc. God is the integral unity of the archetypal masculine and feminine principles.

Then again there is a natural affection in the human heart for children. Love of children is universal. It can be religiously transformed. One can turn to God as the eternal child, embodying simplicity, spontaneity, freshness, joy, freedom and truth. One can also be devoted to the service of children as pure manifestations of the Divine. The archetypal image of the divine child is to be found in most of the religions and mythologies of the world. Mystics long for the divine child to be born in their inner consciousness. The birth of the divine child in man symbolizes the bursting of the light of truth in the human mind or the emergence of a spiritually transfigured personality. The concept of divine incarnation (avatara)—the spirit made flesh—plays a significant part in providing religious orientation to man's deep love and longing for the child. When God is believed to be manifested on earth as a child, like baby Krsna or baby Jesus, man has an opportunity of lavishing his affections upon God revealed as the Son of Man. This is called vatsalya bhava.

Finally, there is the strongest of all instinctual-emotional drives in human nature, namely, the erotic impulse. All other emotions may get swallowed up in it. All other feelings and impulses may be constellated round the erotic impulse as their nucleus. It is well known that complete satisfaction in this world of the erotic impulse is extremely rare, if not impossible. Passion in man is insatiable. Hence the vast importance of religious sublimation. Without some spiritual orientation of elemental human emotions, the restlessness of the human spirit can become terribly devastating. Religion orientation of the erotic impulse is known as *madhura bhava*.

The yoga of love involves spiritual transformation of the erotic impulse. A religious seeker, whether male or female, may look upon himself as a bride in relation to God. From the spiritual standpoint, God is the one supreme Bridegroom, the universal lover. The goal of religious effort is a kind of mystic marriage (*sangama* or *sammilana*) between the human soul and the universal spirit. The proper religious attitude of the soul is one of utter submission, total and unconditional surrender to the divine will. Many mystics in different parts of the world have approached God in this attitude.[22]

The reorientation of feelings described above entails some measure of detachment from mundane aims insofar as they are recognized as not the true end or the true contact with the ultimate ground of all longing. Such detachment is emphasized by all religions as characteristic of the experience of mystical attainment, and renunciation is encouraged as a means of removing the substitute satisfactions or distractions that may stand in the way of inner transformation. Buddhism, for instance, in spite of not being a particularly ascetic religion in actual practice, emphasizes that an attachment to the senses is the snare that prevents us from attaining enlightenment; nirvana may be defined as the cessation of desires. The man of the world who feels a surge of rebellion against such an ideal should recognize that a reduction of drives and greed is part of an individual's normal development and the attainment of self-satisfaction. Neither this reduction nor the mystic's ideal need entail a turning away from the world. If anything, the religious injunctions are to move *into* the world. For example,

"Love thy neighbor as yourself." Only after the inner fulfillment of religion has taken place may giving stand in the place of craving. Only out of a deep sense of independence and invulnerability can the exhortations of great religious leaders be fulfilled, such as Christ's "Resist not evil" and "If any smite thee on the right cheek, turn the left to him as well"; Buddha's "Conquer hatred with love"; or Mohammed's "Recompense evil, conquer it with good."

Just as right action has historically turned into religious moralism and puritanism (which may be what Marx had in mind when he said that religion was the opium of the people), similarly has the concept of right love been corrupted. There is a great difference between the mere play of imagination and the *realization* that God is the object of one's longings. Such a realization is identical to the experience of being in the presence of God because, to use Pascal's words: "How wouldst thou have sought me hadst thou not known me?" The whole process is not so much a redirecting of desire as a meditation on the object of desire to find its ultimate aim, in the course of which process the appearance of the aim changes: to look not in a different direction, but deeper in the same direction. The way in which love of a man or woman can evolve into love of God, a bhakti yogi would say, is in discovering that this is what it was in the first place, the loved individual being the window through which we could perceive some of the divine radiance.* When we know the true object of our love beyond appearance, we can find it in all beings, and in ourselves. This is the sense of the Gospels' "Love thy neighbor as thyself and God above all things." To the mystic, God is in his neighbor, in himself, and in all things, and to the extent that he can perceive the presence, suchness, Ground of Being, he can rejoice

---

* This thought has been developed in modern times by Charles Williams throughout his works and particularly in his commentary to Dante.[23]

in all things. In such moments where the mystic's feelings of beauty and love deepen to the point of taking on a religious quality, it is not "this" being any more that is loved or enjoyed, but Being, through one of its manifestations or embodiments.

In a way devotionalism is saying that what we really want is what we have, and not realizing this we crave different things we lack. Such a craving is a distortion of our original love. When we find it, we can again love, enjoy, glorify, sanctify existence. The whole of the mystical way, therefore, can be conceived as a discovery of what lies in front of our eyes, just as in the natural development of art appreciation we discover that what sounds or colors say is what *we* want to say out of our innermost selves.

Even though devotionalism as such is dying today the death of its traditional symbols, the cultivation of higher feelings, which was its inner sense, remains alive in art, therapies, education, and social life. Most of them might be encompassed in the notion of peak-experience facilitation.

Peak-experiences are precisely, from one point of view, moments of openness to the experience of higher feelings, and are characterized by a more or less lasting desirable effect upon the individual. Any perfect action seems to be the potential source of a peak-experience,[24] but we know that they may also be facilitated by environmental factors, the grouping together of the adequate people, music, isolation, drugs, or exercises. Peak-experiences frequently occur in encounter groups,[25] and the psychedelic subculture bears witness to the collective thirst for them. The same may be said of the renewed interest in meditation practices and the rising interest in alpha-wave self-regulation.*

* Dr. Joe Kamiya (at the Langley Porter Neuropsychiatric Institute, San Francisco) has demonstrated that persons given an indication of the presence and extent of

THE CATHARTIC WAY

The alternative to the cultivation of higher feelings—peak-experiences—whether in devotional, meditative, T-group settings or other, is what I have termed the cathartic way. Here we find less emphasis on redirecting impulses or modifying feelings and more on expressing and accepting them. We should not be led to think that this is a profound difference, though. Whoever engages in a therapeutic journey of the "accepting" type does so, after all, because of a desire to change—and in fact he does change once he gives up some of his obsession with changing and begins to accept his present state. This is what Dr. Beisser has called "the paradoxical theory of change." [27] The reason for this is not hard to understand. In the first place, the "lower" states which we want to change into "higher" ones are frequently only distorted expressions of the latter. By attending to them we can discover the luminous core of what we want to reject, that which we love behind our petty rage and petty attachments. In this way, unlike in bhakti yoga, no "redirecting" is needed other than that which takes place naturally as a result of enhanced awareness of our inner feelings.*

A second aspect which makes the acceptance of feelings a refining process, is similar to that involved in acting consistently in accordance with preferences. Just as the latter may

---

alpha-wave activity in their electroencephalogram at a particular moment, are more or less able to influence the production of such waves. Persons who have learned to maximize alpha-waves report psychological states akin to those characteristic of meditation. Since alpha-waves are also prominent in the electroencephalographic recordings of yogis and Zen monks in meditation, much interest has arisen in feed-back training as a means of facilitating the changes in consciousness associated with it. The interested reader may find more information on the subject in *On the Psychology of Meditation*, written by Dr. Robert E. Ornstein and myself.[26]

* As a Mahayana Buddhist would say, the awakened one knows the passions to be the *bodhi*.

serve to expose the sterility of a path or the hitherto unquestioned contradictions in a personality, an open expression of the life of feelings may shed light upon the fallacious presuppositions and nonfunctional character of many of these feelings—which would not have become evident had they been withheld and controlled.

If the devotional way is that of getting in touch with higher feelings—sacredness, love, beauty—in a symbolic domain or special settings in order to carry such feelings from there into the domain of everyday life, the cathartic way is the opposite: it focuses upon the *actuality* of life in its pseudomanifestations until, by a deepening in the awareness, that "unitive consciousness" of which Maslow speaks is attained.

THE WAY OF DETACHMENT

In speaking of the domain of action, we saw that along with the pursuit of rightness and the pursuit of spontaneity, there is a third approach—what we called right doing—in which one's attitude toward activity is regarded as more important than the activity itself, and whose salient aspects are consciousness and detachment from the fruits of action. In the domain of feeling, too, we find an equivalent to this latter orientation. Along with the devotional and the cathartic ways of working on feelings, with their respective emphasis on right feeling and expressiveness, we find a third approach, in which the emphasis is on detachment from feeling and intense observation of emotional processes. A measure of detachment is implied in the control of feelings in the devotional ways, and detached observation may also be compatible with the cathartic or expressive approaches. However, the most characteristic manifestation of the way of detachment in the domain of feeling is found in asceticism. The understanding of asceticism has been so distorted by the contempt toward the body and guilt about instinctual promptings which have become part of historical religions, that it is hard to discuss its true function as an *exercise* any more. From one point of view, asceticism may be understood as the expression of a hierarchical conception of the organization of actions and drives. The ascetic attempts to bring into operation his higher mental functions through the challenge of will against pain. Since the training in mastery to which he subjects himself is inseparable from the cultivation of a detachment from body and feelings, I will be speaking of the philosophy of asceticism in Chapter IV of this book, where I discuss detachment in greater detail. As for the more concrete applications of the ascetic way, I comment upon them in the section of this chapter that deals with physical avenues to consciousness expansion (pp. 106–115).

The Ways of Knowledge

Just as our feelings determine our actions, our thoughts direct our feelings. This we are not always willing to acknowledge, for it seems to contradict our frequent experience of witnessing a quarrel between our head and our heart. But not all our thinking is conscious, and our heart too "has reasons that reason knoweth not."

We are coming to a period of disillusionment as to the power of thought in shaping man's behavior perhaps because we do not realize that it is precisely the power of wrong thought that has caused the calamities that confront us. This is how Socrates saw it when he said that all evil stems from ignorance. Or Jesus: "Forgive them for they know not what they do." Or Buddha, who saw all suffering ultimately as the fruit of delusion or lack of spiritual vision (*avidya*). Hence the importance assigned to understanding and to the teaching of the truth by those who have striven to change men for the better.

The assumption that knowledge can have an effect on being is not only to be found in religion and moral philosophies, but in humanism and the cultivation of the humanities in our school curricula as well. So much so, that education as a whole is mostly restricted to the area of knowledge and, more particularly, to verbal information.

Yet, every stick has two ends. Just as the way of action can deteriorate into estranged doing and blind submission, and that of devotion into emotional plays of the imagination guided by conformity, so the way of knowing finds its degeneration in dogmatism, empty erudition, and one-sided intellectualism. It is important, therefore, to see how knowledge has been regarded and used as a way of growth.

First of all, it may be well to clarify what we mean by knowledge. The very word *knowing* (or *knowledge*) is one for which many languages have two terms of quite different roots and meanings: *savoir-connaître, saber-conocer, sapere-conoscere, wissen-kennen.* Aldous Huxley, in an essay on knowledge and understanding, proposes that we use the former term for the amassing of information and the latter for a more direct apprehension of reality that engages our feelings as well as our reasoning:

> Knowledge is always in terms of concepts and can be passed on by means of words of other symbols. Understanding is not conceptual, and therefore cannot be passed on. It is an immediate experience, and immediate experience can only be talked about (very inadequately), never shared. Nobody can actually feel another's pain or grief, another's love or joy or hunger. And similarly nobody can experience another's understanding of a given event or situation. There can, of course, be knowledge of such an understanding, and this knowledge may be passed on in speech or writing, or by means of other symbols. Such communicable knowledge

is useful as a reminder that there have been specific understandings in the past, and that understanding is at all times possible. But we must always remember that knowledge of understanding is not the same thing as the understanding, which is the raw material of that knowledge. It is as different from understanding as the doctor's prescription for penicillin is different from penicillin.[28]

Such a use of the term *knowledge* is by no means universal, but Huxley's distinction is important in drawing our attention to the existence of different ways or degrees of knowing, whatever the names we want to give them. Thus, when a mystic speaks of knowing he is definitely not speaking of intellectual knowledge but of a realization or seeing of the truth. This is a function of intuition rather than reason, for in intuitive thinking, as the word indicates, we go *into* things, while reasoning can only be *about* things. Chesterton was drawing a distinction between intuitive and discursive thinking when he said that the poet only asks to get his head into the heavens, but the logician seeks to get heaven into his head (and it is his head that splits). Direct knowledge is not something mysterious and "out of this world" but precisely the opposite: it starts with the knowledge conveyed by our senses and it extends beyond sense-impressions into the totality of our experience. If we stop and reflect on what is the meaning of *knowing* how to play an instrument, *knowing* a language, and particularly *knowing* a certain person, we may realize that such experiential knowledge cannot be conveyed by words. Moreover, as Korzybski emphasizes, no experience can ever be conveyed by words and, therefore, no knowledge.

The apprehension of reality that many philosophies and religions refer to as an aspect of man's full status and ideal condition is in the nature of such direct knowledge drawn to its limit, and not in that of an extension of our conceptual model of the world. In our impatience to know we usually build up theories that are supposed to guide us to reality, but that more often obstruct our view of it or substitute for it. In view of this "concept monster" some traditions have taken on an anti-intellectual style that is repugnant to many intellectuals. For example, we read in the *Hsinhsinming*,[29] the treatise of Zen's third patriarch:

> Do not seek for the truth,
> only stop having an opinion.

Or:

> If the mind makes no discriminations,
> all things are as they really are.

Or:

> The more talking and thinking
> the farther from the truth.

Nicholas of Cusa, in the letter that serves as introduction to his book, *Of Learned Ignorance,* states: ". . . I was led in the learning that is ignorance to grasp the incomprehensible; and this I was able to achieve not by way of comprehension but by *transcending those perennial truths that can be recalled by reason.*"[30] *

THE WAY OF FAITH

It would be inexact to say that the way of knowledge is one of irrationality, for often precisely those who insist on the ineffability of the truth have taken pains to express it in oral, written, or artistic forms, hoping that others might be able to assimilate their words or symbols. Correspondingly, the way of understanding has traditionally consisted in part in the art

* The italics are the author's.

and science of assimilating ideas and symbols. It starts from intellectual understanding and uses it as a blueprint to reach the living understanding of an idea. It is an art of letting ideas sink into life, until they become reality themselves.

The tools of this art are ideas, seed-utterances, or images which take different forms with different traditions: *koans* in Zen, parables and even jokes in dervish *tarikas,* lines from the Scriptures in the Christian world, *mandalas, yantras, mantras* in Tibet, etc. But the art itself is in that form of meditation which consists of examining experience in terms of the model, or becoming absorbed in the model until it shines upon ever-present experience.

There is something that some of the ways of action, feeling, and knowledge we have described have in common: the principle of assimilating an act, a feeling, or an idea *on faith* until it becomes a personal reality, having grown into an understanding. By living *as if* such and such an action were the right one, such and such a feeling or idea the true one, transformation takes place in the individual. Development proceeds, guided by the virtue of key signs and symbols, which derive their power from being rooted in man's shared deeper reality.

Faith, therefore, in its intellectual aspect, amounts to the trusting willingness to accept a road map. It is the willingness to *use* a concept, assuming its truth for the sake of the belief that living according to it will eventually make it a certainty. Such is the understanding of faith, for instance, in Saint Augustine of Hippo: "Understanding is the reward of faith. Therefore do not seek to understand in order that you may believe, but make the act of faith in order that you may understand; for unless you make an act of faith you will not understand." [31]

This process of temporary acceptance of a truth in view of its eventual understanding is by no means unique to metaphysical truths, but is to be seen in any learning and teaching situation. It is in the domain of metaphysical truth, though, that statements of faith (perhaps because of the difficulty of reaching the true understanding) tend to become statements of belief that take the place of the understanding rather than leading to it. And when the map is taken for the reality, one discovers that there are not one but many maps of the same reality, perhaps equally useful to the traveler, but a source of perplexity for the map collector who does not know that there is a reality other than that of their discrepant colors, distances, and names of places.

James Jeans,[32] commenting on how both the wave-interpretation and corpuscle-interpretation of light make it possible to understand certain phenomena which cannot be reconciled in one image, suggests that as in Plato's myth of the cave our rational mind can only grasp a shadow of a greater-dimensioned reality; whatever kind of map we make, it will distort the reality of the earth into a model of fewer dimensions. For example, in an orthogonal projection of the earth's surface we have to sacrifice accuracy in the proportionality of areas, while in a conic projection areas are more realistically depicted but directions are not exact. Thus with the world at large the best approximation of the truth that we can have is a variety of points of view.

It is precisely in terms of the function of conceptual maps that we may understand the difference between the intellectual attitudes of diverse traditions and find the expression of three approaches which intermingle in different proportions, sometimes with a clear-cut preponderance of one or the other.

One of them is the approach that concentrates on the study of a single map: the way of faith. A particular set of symbols is here employed to the exclusion of all others, and this system is contemplated and evinced until it becomes alive with a life of experience projected on to it. The model is perfected until it becomes one with the territory itself, as would be the case if a hypothetical mapmaker came to build a life-size model of the earth out of identical materials. Though the single-map approach is the most likely to deteriorate into fanatical dogma, it cannot be denied that it offers the advantage of concentration: it may be easier to find water by digging one deep well than by spending the same energies in digging several shallow ones.

Then there is the way of questioning and exploring, in which the individual, instead of working from an externally given map into experience, explores the givenness of his experience seeking to translate it into articulate expression; instead of seeking to understand a tradition or respected authority that tells him "here is the truth," he looks into himself, questioning all the ready-made answers. It is the way of creativity, which bypasses dogmas and generates new symbolic forms. In contrast to the way of faith, it is a way of doubt.

> When you have enough faith, then you have enough doubt, and when you have enough doubt, then you have enough satori.
>
> —SHUKO

THE NEGATIVE WAY

Finally, there is the negative approach to knowledge, which emphasizes that the map is *not* the territory.* Paradox or apparently irrational statements may be used, as in Zen, or the Sufi method called "scatter": a juxtaposition of formulations, the internal unity of which is not apparent but must be grasped at a nonliteral level of understanding—the use of dissimilar maps. But the essential aspect of this approach is not in

---

* This view is the opposite of that of the way of faith which encourages projection and where the subject fades away in the object, and man in God; in the negative approach (for instance in Zen or gnani yoga) the object is reabsorbed into the subject and merges into the self.

the road maps but in the specific technique of suppressing thought, or relinquishing (temporarily) all conceptual activity. This is an asceticism of the mind rather than of the feelings or of the body, and centers around the idea that only if we give up our attachment to thoughts and schemes of reality we may become open to a more direct apprehension of what we are. As Edward Carpenter has expressed it:

> Of all the hard facts of Science . . . I know of none more solid and fundamental than the fact that if you inhibit thought (and persevere) you come at length to a region of consciousness below or behind thought, and different from ordinary thought in its nature and character—a consciousness of quasi-universal quality, and a realization of an altogether vaster self than that to which we are accustomed. And since the ordinary consciousness, with which we are concerned in ordinary life, is before all things founded on the little local self, and is in fact *self*-consciousness in the little local sense, it follows that to pass out of that is to die to the ordinary self and the ordinary world.
>
> It is to die in the ordinary sense, but in another sense it is to wake up and find that the "I," one's real, most intimate self, pervades the universe and all other beings—that the mountains and the sea and the stars are a part of one's body and that one's soul is in touch with the souls of all creatures. . . .
>
> So great, so splendid is this experience, that it may be said that all minor questions and doubts fall away in face of it; and certain it is that in thousands and thousands of cases the fact of its having come even once to a man has completely revolutionized his subsequent life and outlook on the world.[33]

Beyond the general statement that an intuition of reality transcends reasoning, the suspension of thought constitutes a form of meditation described in various traditions. The following description of the exercise is taken from W. Y. Evans-Wentz's compilation of Tibetan yoga texts and appears under the heading "The Inhibiting of the Thought Process."

The cutting-off of a thought at the root the very moment, as in a flash, it ariseth, is practiced as followeth:

In meditating, in the manner above explained, one findeth that, because of the mind responding to stimuli, thoughts crop up continuously. Knowing that the birth of even a single idea should be prevented, one must try to inhibit this continuous cropping up of thoughts, by exercise of mental alertness. Thus, as soon as a thought sprouteth, try to chop it down, root and all, and continue meditating.

By prolonging, during the meditation, the period of time in which the effort is made to prevent the arising of thoughts, one finally cometh to be aware of thoughts following close on the heels of one another so numerous that they seem interminable. This is the recognizing of thoughts, which equalleth the knowing of the enemy. It is called "The First Resting Place," the first stage of mental quiescence attained; and the *yogin* then looketh on, mentally unperturbed, at the interminable flow of thoughts as though he were tranquilly resting on the shore of a river watching the water flow past.

Once the mind attaineth the tranquil state, for even the briefest moment, it understandeth the arising and the cessation of thoughts. This understanding maketh one to feel as though thoughts were becoming more and more numerous, but, really, thoughts are always arising and there is neither increase nor decrease of them. Thoughts are born instantaneously. That which is apart from and capable of immediately arresting this birth of thoughts is the Reality.

Later, under the heading "The Non-Reacting to Thoughts," the text continues:

In the next practice, the leaving unshaped whatever concept or idea appeareth, the procedure is to be indifferent to the thought, allowing it to do as it liketh, neither falling under its influence, nor attempting to impede it. Let the mind act as its shepherd (or watchman); and go on meditating.[34]

It is only natural to expect that those who have had access to a knowledge not attained by reflecting upon symbols, parables, or theologies, will deem these as relatively unimportant. We can therefore understand the anti-intellectual tendency of most mystics, the disregard of some traditions for the written word (e.g., *The Bauls of Bengal*), and a sentiment toward the Holy Scriptures wholly different from the Christian or Brahmanical veneration. Illustrative of this attitude is the story of a keeper of the Buddhist scriptures who, noticing a Zen monk sitting silently for some time in the library, asked him why he did not read the Sutras. As the monk answered that he did not know the letters, the librarian went on to inquire why he did not ask to be taught. The monk replied to this advice by pointing at his chest and saying, "Please tell me what character this is." [35]

The pointing at the self, or at the heart, in this story is the opposite of the way of faith as we have described it. (It is true that faith is a major concept in Buddhism, but not in the sense of faith toward a doctrine but in that of faith in the *dharma* and in the Buddha nature—a *trusting* rather than a believing.) The approach of pointing directly at the mind, as Zen puts it, constitutes a method opposite to that of working into experience from the blueprint symbolic formulation, and which is like the creative path of the artist. The difference lies in that the discipline here is one of suppressing concepts, while in the expressive endeavor it is one of attuning concepts to reality.

In contrast to two of the approaches outlined above—the assimilation of symbolic forms (the way of faith) and the elimination of conceptual activity (the negative way)—stands a third form of development in the sphere of understanding. I briefly referred to it already as a way of doubt and inquiry.* I

* See p. 92.

call it the "creative way" for it is the solitary path of many an artist.

THE CREATIVE WAY

The creative approach shares an "experientialistic" emphasis with the negative way but differs from it in its reliance upon individuality and discovery, an attitude that runs parallel to the affirmative, nonascetic, and nondisciplinarian approach to action. For the latter too stems from a belief that "all desires are ultimately expressions of God's will," and the individual will find what is right for him without need of fetters. The creative way goes hand in hand, too, with the parallel approach in the domain of feelings of noninterventionist self-expression (the opposite of devotionalism) which relies on the principle that the hidden feeling-truth of the individual will naturally actualize itself if it is only let out in an atmosphere of nonjudgmental acceptance. These three approaches taken together constitute what the Hindus have sometimes called the left-hand path. One of its assumptions is that, by further developing his most developed aspect, the individual will come to the point of overflow and reach beyond his present state. Instead of striving for transformation, the person is here prompted to accept what he is and follow his trend. "Cease striving," said Chuang Tzu, "and self-transformation will ensue." It is a philosophy of trust in self-nature, of surrender to the developmental wisdom of the organism, a spirit of feasting rather than fasting, as exemplified by the Hasidic Jews with their music and dancing, and in the rites of Tantric yoga. It is a "democratic" approach in that it holds that "the kingdom of heaven" is for everyone to find in his own heart and that the way is for each to find for himself. "The ways are as many as the breaths in a man," runs a Sufi saying.

I think that it is quite clear that this left-hand path is the characteristic style of our times. Dynamic psychology from its beginning had some of this character in its concern with impulse expression and its trust in the fact that change depends more on the patient's expression of himself than on external advice. From here, psychotherapy has been moving more and more away from the interpretive aspects of psychoanalysis, and from thinking in general, into an interest in the body.* Education, too, to the extent that it is "experimental," moves in the direction of greater trust in the autonomous development of the child; in the arts, traditional patterns are being left aside; and in the religious domain there is a growing interest in the ways that do not provide answers but mainly means for one to find them.

The Ways of Mindfulness

Thinking is, of man's instruments, the most relevant to the act of knowing; yet the aim of knowing is beyond thinking, for it is the prerogative of the knower in us: our self, or, if we like, our consciousness. The same may be said of the rest of the human mechanism. Doing may be a way of self-development, but the end of such development is not the programing of the human apparatus to this or that set of actions, but the development of the self; that is, the doer. The self cannot be divorced from its functions but, paradoxically, doing, feeling, and thinking may become automatic operations divorced from the self. This is why the ways to the growth of the self may be regarded, from one point of view, as conducive to making all our activities our own—bringing ourselves into them rather than being alienated from our actions, feelings, and thoughts. Selfhood

* This interest is prominent, for instance, in Lowen's bioenergetic analysis,[36] in Gestalt therapy,[37] and in the less systematic corpus of encounter techniques.

gives every domain a transforming touch, as we know from our peak-experiences and as we are told by those who have been so deeply touched by them that they felt inclined to express them in art, words, or deeds. Selfhood implies will; that is, the experience of one's self as the doer. This is what Helmuth Kaiser was concerned with when he claimed that neurotic patients are less responsible than normal individuals:

> My contention is that patients, according to the degree of their illness—however one may determine it—are far less "behind" their words and actions than healthy persons. This is the same phenomenon which is usually referred to by the statement that neurotics are less well integrated than healthy persons. The rifts in the neurotic's personality do not permit him to be "present" to the same degree in his actions and words as are healthier personalities. As a somewhat crude example: a comparatively healthy person will, even when yielding to a severe threat, retain the feeling that he made a decision—that he preferred to do what he was asked to do rather than suffer the punishment. A severely neurotic person of a certain type, on the other hand, will be inclined—even when only a request was voiced, unaccompanied by a threat—to feel: I have no choice.
>
> There are neurotics who have to experience every major desire in their lives as something completely determined by circumstances. While the healthy person would say that the decision was easy, that the pros by far outweighed the cons, these neurotics say, "Fate decided for me: I had no choice." Both groups might do the same under the same circumstances, might even recognize and weigh the pros and cons exactly alike but their feeling is different. Other types of neurotics feel "I did it, but I did not want to do it." Or, "I wanted to do it, but at the same time I did not want to do it." What the neurotic feels about his actions also holds true for the words he speaks. The words are his and he knows it, but the meaning is not quite his—not undisputably really and truly his.[38]

Selfhood, in the domain of feeling, is expressed in the gratui- tous joy and love that mystics have expressed throughout cen- turies. And in thinking, selfhood first of all implies independ- ent thought; just as will and freedom operate in external actions, in the internal process of thinking "the thinker" be- comes able to choose his own thoughts and tell them apart from the superimposed thinking of others. Thus thoughts be- come an independent translation of our contact with experi- ence. A person who "comes to himself" as a result of psycho- therapy or other experiences may find that his vision of the world is changed, and that what he formerly regarded as his thoughts were only grafts from parents or significant others, which have become automatized. Such "seeing with one's own eyes" is essentially a function of consciousness, which is then interpreted, translated, and elaborated on by thinking.

Perhaps of all our faculties consciousness is the most self- bound. Nobody but the "I" in each of us can be conscious. In- deed, some metaphysical views hold that the self is conscious- ness and nothing but consciousness.

Thinkers like Teilhard de Chardin and Aurobindo Ghose present us with a picture of the whole cosmic evolution as an evolution of consciousness, or an evolution toward conscious- ness. Whether we want to accept such a view or not, we cannot fail to see that our own evolution as a species and as individ- uals is that of an expanding consciousness of ourselves and the world. Education is, at least from one point of view, a widen- ing of the individual's consciousness of his inner and outer world, and much of psychotherapy, too, may be seen as a res- toration of consciousness.

I have been thinking of the word *mindfulness* rather than consciousness in the heading of this section to stress the act of consciousness which is one of being conscious of something. For this reason, the way of consciousness cannot be separated from the three ways of action, feeling, and knowing. Furthermore, if any of the three ways is divorced from this fourth, it ceases to be a way of growth, and becomes a matter of molding the personality in a given way. Thus, in the domain of activity, while seeking the conformity of action to our ideal, or to a given task, or to our truest inclination, we cannot avoid being conscious. Consciousness will spring from the friction of the task at hand with our desires; and consciousness, too, will be needed to ascertain our desires. Only mechanical action can be unconscious, and therefore without significance as a way. It is a corollary of this principle that the procedures surveyed in this study have in common the trait of demanding of a person something outside the limits of his customary activity. If every right action were to become traditional and mechanical (as among the Pharisees as presented in the Gospels) it would cease to be a challenge and a way of growth, whatever its social value.

The following Sufi story is especially expressive of the notion of an added dimension of being out of which action can derive its ultimate effectiveness and without which it becomes just an irrelevant event:

Two pious and worthy men went into a mosque together. The first one took off his shoes and placed them neatly, side by side, outside the door. The second man removed his shoes, placed them sole to sole, and took them into the mosque with him.

There was an argument among a group of other pious and worthy folk who were sitting at the door, as to which of these men was the better. "If one went barefoot into a mosque, was it not better to leave the very shoes outside?" asked one. "But should we not consider," said another, "that the man who took his shoes into the mosque carried them to remind himself by their very presence that he was in a state of proper humility?"

When the two men came out after their prayers, they were

questioned separately, as it happened, by different parties from the onlookers.

The first man said: "I left my shoes outside for the usual reason. The reason is that if anyone wants to steal them he will have an opportunity of resisting that temptation, and thus acquiring merit for himself." The listeners were most impressed by the highmindedness of a man whose possessions were of so little account to him that he willingly entrusted them to whatever might be their fate.

The second man, at the same time, was saying: "I took my shoes into the mosque because, had I left them outside, they might have constituted a temptation to steal them. Whoever had yielded to this temptation would have made me his accomplice in sin." The hearers were most impressed by this pious sentiment, and admired the thoughtfulness of the sage.

But yet another man, a man of wisdom, who was present, cried out: "While you two men and your followers have been indulging in your admirable sentiment, training each other with the play of hypothetical instances, certain *real* things have been happening."

"What were these things?" asked the crowd.

"Nobody was tempted by the shoes. Nobody was not tempted by the shoes. The theoretical sinner did not pass by. Instead, another man altogether, who had no shoes at all to carry with him or to leave outside, entered the mosque. Nobody noticed his conduct. He was not conscious of the effect which he might be having on people who saw him or did not see him. But, because of his real sincerity, his prayers in this mosque today helped, in the most direct way possible, all the potential thieves who might or might not steal shoes or reform themselves by being exposed to temptation."

Do you still not see that the mere practice of self-conscious conduct however excellent in its own realm, is a pale thing indeed when measured against the knowledge that there are real men of wisdom? [39]

The image of praying here aptly conveys the intangible nature of the element that is missing from the actions of carrying the shoes or not. In terms of self-development, it is not going left or right that counts, but the act of consciousness required by both.

The practice of simple awareness in all the activities of daily life is very much stressed in certain traditions. Idries Shah has listed eleven rules of the Naqshbandi Order of the Sufis, and we can see that several bear on the question of attention directed toward the obvious and immediate: "awareness of breathing," "watching the feet," "remembering," "awareness of distractions." This is also the spirit of physical work in Zen monasteries. "The dialogues and discussions," writes Suzuki, "were most intimately connected with life itself. Each pulsation of the heart, the lifting of the hands and feet, all evoked considerations of the most serious character. For this is the only way to study Zen and to live it. Nothing can ever really be learned until it works through the nerves and muscles." [40]

The following fragment of an article by Phiroz Mehta gives a good picture of the implications of mindfulness in Buddhist practice:

> Repentance, the turning away from worldliness, is hardly possible without seeing that from which one must turn away. Therefore observe action and speech and the flow of thought and feeling from moment to moment. Continuous watchfulness, impossible in the early stages, becomes an established awakened condition even when asleep (see the *Majjhima Nikaya*, I. 249), through constant practice.
>
> One must be a fully observant witness without censure or approval, without aversion or attraction. Censure can give rise to a guilt complex with all its undesirable concomitants, and approval can lead to pride and complacency. Neither a guilt complex nor pride is conducive to freedom from the ego-sense. Nor is aversion or attraction, each of which indicates that that which is observed is master of the observer. Censure, approval, aversion and attraction all prevent calm and freedom, vision and insight.

The profound depths of the mind are vested with the peace and harmony which are healing powers of egoless being. Directing calm attention to the surface states of the psyche transforms them. Just as the physical cells of the living body are characterized by the power of self-healing, there is, so to say, a self-righting tendency in the psyche. A physical wound is dressed or a fatigued man rests in order to have a chance for a restoration to health. So too, there is a chance for the restoration of the psyche to holiness when the surface disturbances of the mind is "treated" by calm observation.

Mindfulness acquaints one with oneself. Great courage is needed in order to persevere with this practice, for the self-revelation invariably shocks one and much emotional and intellectual distress is experienced. When courage fails, energy flags, the enormity of the task crushes one, depression envelops one like a black thundercloud, the terror of the unknown depths of the soul and the fear caused by seeing what one does see even in the early stages overwhelm one, do not cry for help, nor fly to a friend for consolation, nor delve into a book of wisdom. Keep quiet, or else one is sure to get hurt. Simply look. Under the compassionate gaze of the sleepless immortal eyes, the confusion of the mind and the turmoil in the heart come to rest. . . .

Above all, fantasies clearly reveal inward morality. Watch the fantasies of hate and anger—the terrible things one does to the hated one! Watch the fantasies of lust for power, possessions, sex, personal superiority, doing good, becoming perfect, serving God and putting the whole world right! Watch the fantasies of all the subtle forms of indulgence, artistic and intellectual, sporting and exhilarating; and of planning out the lives of one's own children, and of others not so close! . . .

Paying complete attention to the whole situation is true mindfulness. For this, it is necessary to be free of all beliefs, of all the burden of the past, of all authorities. For any belief, on however great an authority it is based, is an assumption. Hence one's own mind is unfree. And the unfree mind cannot see truth. Any patient person will see the tremendous implications of this. Who so aspires, and dares, may realize the immeasurable. There is no authoritative instruction to give or ideal to follow. There is no particular way. Yet, seek out the way—your own way. Every way which is a borrowed or dictated way comes at last to a dead-end. But your own way—and you *are* a self responsible, unique individual in reality—is the way which allows you continual emergence. Your own way is no other than your own mindfulness. It is the way of everlasting life, of sweet savour, without a moment of stinking stagnation.[41]

Since mindfulness can only be mindfulness of an ongoing experience, the way of consciousness is the same as that of self-insight, which became explicit in our Western civilization at the time of Socrates' injunctions of self-examination, and has culminated in the institution of psychotherapy.

Mindfulness to daily events and inner states is the embodiment of the way of consciousness in ordinary life, as precepts and faith constitute embodiment of the ways of action, feeling, and knowledge. Just as in the other three ways, there is place for special exercises (rituals, prayers, and meditation, for instance) that are especially intended for the development of attention and consciousness. These might be collectively called meditation even though some forms of meditation may involve an intellectual, affective, or physical operation aside from the exercising of awareness. Though there seems to be no complete agreement as to exact definitions and boundaries, the practice of meditation may be generally considered to be subdivided into three distinct sets of exercises.

One type of meditation is essentially concentrative, and therefore eliminative; the main effort here is to withdraw attention from everything but the meditation object. This is the expression, in the domain of meditation practice, of the negative way, and involves an exercising of the will. A second type of practice is the expression of the same tendency manifested in the ways of right action, devotion ritual, and faith. In this type of meditation, the meditator seeks to identify with a meditation object to the point of self-forgetfulness. (An instance of this is cited on pp. 224–25.)

What may be regarded as the purest type of meditation, though, in the sense of its being purely an exercise in awareness, is that in which the meditation object is no other than the spontaneous flow of experience at the moment, including the special state of consciousness which may arise where consciousness abides in itself. This type of practice is sometimes referred to as contemplation.

In contrast to the previous types, which are structured, in contemplation the aim of the practice is the giving up of structure and standing aside from the unfolding of one's spontaneity.

The three dimensions of meditation may be found again as dimensions in some of the present-day psychological approaches. The negative efforts aiming at a stilling of the mind and at a state of concentrated, undistracted receptivity, is best represented in relaxation techniques such as Johannes Schultz's autogenic training.[42] Meditation upon externally given objects or images constitutes an important part of psychosynthesis.[43] Even though he did not give it the name of meditation, Minor White has recently described a way of extending perception through photography, which falls into the same type of exercise.[44] The practice of pure awareness is the central exercise in Gestalt therapy, having in this therapeutic system a role comparable to that of free association in psychoanalysis.[45] This exercise involves the three efforts outlined above in different proportions—concentration on the actual, suppression of conceptual activity, and noninterference in the flow of experience.

In general, it may be said that here, as in the domains of action, feeling, and thinking, it is the left-hand path and the negative way that dominate the contemporary scene. The rediscovery of awareness that has taken place in recent years, as evidenced by sensory awareness, sensory awakening, sensitivity training, Gestalt therapy, psycholitic psychotherapy, and popular interest in za-zen, is mostly expressed in forms that are an invitation to relinquish forms, and convey a trust in consciousness as the real transforming power beyond all formulas.

Physical Avenues to Consciousness Enhancement

Any boundary between the physical and the psychological cannot fail to be artificial, and yet the predominantly physical ways deserve separate attention because of their historical importance.

The history of man's striving for perfection is closely related to asceticism. The word *asceticism* derives from the Greek *askesis* meaning exercise, training. Just as the athlete was physically trained, so he was trained in the virtues. That spiritual development takes specific efforts and practices seems to have been recognized as early as prehistoric times.

Asceticism conceived in such broad terms would naturally embrace all that has been covered in the foregoing pages, being equivalent to the subject matter of this book. Yet, in practice, the word asceticism has come to designate a specific trend in the domain of spiritual exercises: the negative way, the way of sacrifice, austerity, and abstinence. It entails on one hand the deprivation of all that may institute a source of pleasure—food, shelter, rest and sleep, sex, company and conversation, power, choice—reflected in the monastic vows of poverty, obedience, and chastity. On the other hand it entails the deliberate inflicting of pain—physical (flagellation) or psychological (humiliation). These methods are by no means confined to Christian monasticism but are to be found in practically all religions and in shamanism. It should be noted that asceticism cannot be equated with religion, that both the Buddha and Jesus Christ taught moderation, and that in the Parsis' *Vendidad* it is said that "he who fills himself with meat is filled with the good spirit more than he who does not do so."

Are we to consider asceticism a matter of superstition or, at best, questionable opinions, and a consequence of masochism and guilt, or, rather, as a practice that may have a desirable psychological effect? We tend to think of asceticism as the corollary of the concept that all which pertains to the body, the senses and their satisfaction is evil, and therefore has to be given up, and we look at such a concept with suspicion, as being antiphysiological to say the least. Yet, we find that asceticism as a penitential activity developed later in religious history than (and probably as a consequence of the deterioration of) an earlier asceticism which aimed solely at the achievement of detachment (transcendence) and will, or mastery over physical and emotional needs. Earlier than that we find ascetic practices in almost all primitive cultures, including those whose value systems have no place for the sinfulness of the flesh.

It is in primitive cultures precisely that we can most clearly discern a functional significance of ascetic practices, later forgotten as the instruments of fire-making came to be adored for themselves. In such cultures ascetic ordeals are generally associated with initiations—with initiations into adulthood in particular, and most clearly with the initiation of shamans.

Fasting, for instance, in the contemporary civilized world is prescribed by some religions at appointed times in the year, and might be described as customary or traditional. In Christianity it is the residue of the penitential fasting of some centuries ago, which in turn evolved from preparatory fasting preceding festive days. Such fasts during the second century had as their object "to temper the mind, lest contrary affections coming in place should make it too profuse and dissolute." These preparatory fastings might then be considered analogous in nature to those preceding the ordination of monks in the Christian middle ages. But here we also find wider correspondences. In the Greek mysteries of Eleusis, for instance, the mystic went into a fast that preceded the eating and drinking of sacramental food. Clement of Alexandria has preserved the words spoken by the initiated: "I have fasted, I have drunk the cyceon." Something similar can be said of the Mithraic ritual, of the Athenian Thesmophoria, of the Roman cult of Ceres. And we are rather discouraged from making a purely cultural interpretation of such fasts by the finding of similar acts of preparation among the Peruvians before the conquest (on occasion of the festival of the summer solstice), the Lapp sorcerers before offering sacrifice, the Cherokee Indians before slaying the sacred eagle.

The pervasiveness of preparatory and initiatory fasts suggests by itself that the deprivation of food and the exercise of self-restraint involved in such deprivation may indeed elicit states of mind that are considered appropriate for (or the goal of) the festivals, sacraments, or sacrifices. This becomes more clear when we examine the details of the natives' practices.

We find that young men of the Mesquakie Indians, for instance, undergo a nine-year training, which becomes steadily more severe. "The fasts that at first were deprivation from one meal lengthen, till they stretch over days and nights of abstinence from both food and water." Finally comes the nine-day fast, during which the lad wanders in the woods and has feverish dreams, in one of which he learns what his "medicine" is to be.[46] Charlevoix describes the privations of the young tribesmen among the Algonquins and others: "They begin by blackening the boy's face, then they cause him to fast for eight days without giving him anything to eat." This induces dreams which are carefully inquired into. "Nevertheless the fast often ends before the proper time, as few lads can keep it up so long." Among those undergoing apprenticeship as shamans, fasting is a preparatory act to the reception of higher knowledge and, as some of the following instances show, it is dreams that are regarded the vehicle of revelation.

The Eskimo youth who wishes to become an *angekok* must retire and fast for some time until he achieves visions, in which the spirits are supposed to visit him.[47] Among the Lapps, those who wished to be wizards had to fast strictly.[48] In Brazil, the youth who desires to be a *paje* dwells alone and fasts often over a period of two years, after which he is admitted as a *paje*.[49] Among the Abipones, the postulant for the position of *keebit* had to sit on a tree overhanging a lake for some days, fasting, until he began to see into the future.[50] Similar methods were practiced among the North American tribes in order to become a medicine man. These included very severe and prolonged fastings, which were followed by vivid dreams. And among the Zulus diviners become qualified for their work and for communication with spirits by a severe discipline which extends over a protracted period and includes very rigorous fasting. Thus the youth becomes a house of dreams.[51]

This significance of fasting, which might be called functional or instrumental, has been recognized throughout all lands and times, but has usually been obscured by its understanding as a meritorious act or a rite. Galen, for instance, notes that dreams produced by fasting are clearer than others, which coincides with a proverb among Zulu diviners to the effect that "the continually stuffed body cannot see secret things." MacCulloch suggests that the Chinese custom of fasting before a sacrifice to the ancestral spirits may have had the intention of causing communion with them through visions. The Pythia, the oracle of Delphi, also fasted as a preparation for her inspiration (in addition to chewing laurel and inhaling the vapors that filled the grotto). In Tertullian's opinion, fasting gives rise to dreams and Chrysostom states that it makes the soul brighter and provides it with wings to mount and soar.

Many of the above-quoted statements on the effects of fasting, such as the elicitation of vivid dreams or visions, the brightening of the soul, etc., suggest that the essential process behind them may be in the nature of an increased access to consciousness of what normally lies in the domain of unconscious perception, feeling, or fantasy. If such is the case, fasting evidently deserves exploration in an experimental context that may prove the point. The same may be said of the other ascetic practices used in conjunction with fasting in some of the examples cited above. It is hard at times to decide the relative weight of each technique on the alleged effects, but a case might be made for their functional significance aside from local beliefs and customs.

Some exploratory work in recent years suggests a revival of some of the ascetic ways, intentional or not. As in shamanistic or monastic practice, it is hard to assess the total contribution of given procedures that are only a component of a complex system, and we can assume that such a component is only part of the whole. Physical pain, for instance, is a component of the post-Reichian approach, as typified by Alexander Lowen. I personally wonder to what extent sheer pain is responsible for some of the subjective and physical effects of Ida Rolf's postural realignment. The practice of opening up to painful stimuli and remaining relaxed in their presence can conceivably modify a person's attitude and perception of the body in general. Sleep deprivation, too, is being used quite often in conjunction with group psychotherapy in the so-called marathon setting. Extremes of exertion are advocated as an educational venture leading to peak-experiences. The most complete example of deprivation from sensory stimuli is probably the isolation chamber designed by Dr. John Lilly which, as this investigator claims, can induce peak-experiences in adequately prepared subjects.[52]

The negative way of self-torture by no means covers the entire field of the physical approaches to human development. Its affirmative counterpart is in the way of facilitating the unfolding of the body's natural tendencies. Yet this would not possibly constitute a way of growth if it were completely "natural" for the body to be natural. Implicit in the notion of an approach to the organic rightness of movements, posture, and breathing is the view that the condition of average humanity is one of wrongness in these elementary activities.

This position is put forward in very articulate manner by F. Matthias Alexander, for instance, who out of self-experimentation created a system and school still better known in England than in the United States (except for the writings of Alexander[53] and his pupil John Dewey). Alexander stresses that not only do we stand, walk, sit, talk wrongly (i.e., in a nonfunctional, contrived way) but our feeling of what is physically right is also wrong, being dictated by habit. The practitioner of this system, therefore, subjects a person to gentle but persistent manipulation to the effect of awakening a latent but suppressed sense of rightness in posture and simple activities until an enduring change can take place.

At this point we may ask ourselves what can be the value of one posture over another, for instance, or what can the relevance be of this kind of physical discipline for the ways of growth as we have been conceiving them. An answer to this may be found in considering such physical ways as extensions of the principle of right doing, and relevant to "the doctrine of the perfect act." In this view it is not an action in itself, physical or not, that counts; the perfecting of the process of the doing is a challenge that can only be met by a perfection in the doer. Looking at the latter from a slightly different angle, we can also see in right posture an extension of right action and the principle that by enacting certain forms a person may be more receptive to certain attitudes which are like the spirit of the form. We know that certain words, for instance, are translated automatically into our posture and style of movement. We can therefore conceive that as these postures become habitual and automatic, as everything physical tends to become, our inner states will also become fixed in a psychophysical interdependence. Liberating the body of habit in favor of a flexible adjustment to the situations of the moment could in this way give increased freedom to the mind.

Not only do negative inner states lead to "faulty postures," but there is reason to believe that unusual states of higher consciousness have their physical correlates too. Just as Jung points out the archetypical quality of certain images (in art, myth, dreams) that seems to emerge from the unconscious without having been assimilated from the culture, we might also understand the various *mudras* and *asanas* of yoga, for instance, as natural concomitants of certain inner states. In adopting such postures a person is acting *as if* he were in the given state; thus he may be more open to it, and it is natural that they should be recommended as the starting points for meditation. What has been said of yogic postures may be applied, too, to the Chinese discipline of *tai chi chuan* and other Eastern disciplines of movement. Isolated aspects of all these survive in our culture either as customs or because they are rediscovered again and again by those who are involved in sports or dance. For instance, the insistence of British schoolteachers on having the children "sit up straight" seems like an echo of the ancient recognition that "a straight back breeds straight thoughts," and it may be noted that the position of the body and feet in the Japanese martial arts or in *tai chi chuan* is the same that an expert tennis or fencing coach would recommend.

A third way to consider the physical avenues to human development is that of chemical or metabolic means. This discussion overlaps with the one of austerities because fasting involves a modification of body chemistry and sleep deprivation probably affects brain metabolism, but we will not do more than point out these effects. A more specific way of affecting body chemistry is by means of the suppression of breathing, as practiced in advanced stages of hatha yoga. The technique employed in that tradition involves the swallowing of one's tongue (to inhibit the breathing reflex) after this has been stretched by months of exercise, massage, and section of the frenum. Several minutes of interrupted breathing are required for the induction of an ecstatic experience which is only possible for a person with the required psychological preparation.

The inhibition of breathing has the effect described in yoga literature probably because of the accumulation of carbon dioxide in the bloodstream, which is easy now to cause artificially with no deleterious effect. A form of treatment for psychological disturbances which consists in the breathing of an oxygen-carbon dioxide mixture was in fact introduced by Ladislas J. Meduna and has not received much attention since the appearance of his book.[54] It would be understandable that a rise in the CO_2 content of the blood could transitorily interfere with the operation of ego functions and thus permit the conscious expression of other aspects in the person's psyche.

Drugs represent still another means of chemical influence upon psychological processes. Primitive cultures in general are very aware of their natural floral pharmacopoeia, and many of the drugs in our pharmacies are either extracts, synthetic analogues, or derivatives of such age-old remedies. Among such drugs in use by Indians of many localities, we are here interested in particular in the group which, like fasting and austerities, tend to induce altered states of consciousness. The common quality of such drugs is best conveyed by the term *psychedelic* proposed by Dr. Humphry Osmond, meaning mind-expanding. Such a quality brings into the focus of awareness aspects of the inner or outer reality that are not normally conscious—a shift in perception that may be experienced as either ecstatic or terrifying according to the context of the situation and the person's psychological condition.

The use of plants containing such mind-changing substances has held a prominent role in certain cultures and, in general, has been associated both with the initiations into adult life and the initiation and training of shamans and medicine men. There is probably a connection between such shamanistic use and the more formulated ritual, sacrificial, or eucharistic drinks mentioned in myths or accounts of early religions. Thus, Robert Gordon Wasson claims that the *haoma* of the *Zend-Avesta* and the *soma* drink of the *Rig Veda* were both made of the hallucinogenic *Amanita muscaria,* still in use among Siberian nomads.[55] The old Egyptians certainly used psychedelic substances, and so did the Greeks, the Persians, the post-Vedic Hindus, and the Chinese. The fourth chapter of Patanjali's *Yoga Sutras* (approximately 500 B.C.) begins: "Supernatural powers are obtained by birth, drugs, power of the word, self-discipline, samadhi." [56]

We have been recently rediscovering the psychedelic substances used by humanity since time immemorial, but there might be occasion to wonder whether our use of them for the purpose of human growth is as comprehensive or sophisticated as that of the old religious or even the "primitive" shamans.* There are indications that such drugs may affect conditioning in a way that somewhat metaphorically has been called reimprinting, and at least one study informs of their deliberate use in the educational setting as an "initiatory" means to awaken potential interests.[58] Huxley, in the utopian view displayed in his last book, *Island,* presents the use of a psychedelic drug as part of a puberty ceremony, in accordance with a widespread Indian usage now well documented by anthropologists.[59]

The Role of Helpers

Just as the whole process of development may be seen as moved by the force of a growth motivation, so too the different approaches may be seen as originating in more specific forms of this drive. It is as though man, in his longing for an invisible goal, had an intuition of it at least, just as in Plato's terms, some men "retain an adequate remembrance" or see "through a glass dimly" the things of another world. William H. Sheldon has shown how men of different constitutions react to distress by seeking action (even if just walking around the block), contact with another, and affection, or in understanding the situation.[60] We might apply the same to the existential preoccupation of feeling unfulfilled, incomplete, always "in the making."

An intuitive prefiguration of possibilities, just as the motives toward action or introspection, leads man at any age to cry for help. The growing individual seeks not only a method or way,

* The recent books *The Teachings of Don Juan* and *A Separate Reality* by Carlos Castaneda present a firsthand account of the shamanistic practices of a Yaqui Indian and strongly suggest that we are still fumbling in areas of experience in which American Indians moved with technical exactness.[57]

but a teacher, an instructor, a guru, a shaman, a psychiatrist.

And, in fact, only artificially can procedures be divorced from the relationship in which they are applied. Furthermore, some of what we would like to consider "systems" are interwoven with the helper's activity in a way that cannot be designated as a role, but only as an unprogramed adventure. For Jung, for instance, "psychotherapy is not the simple straightforward method people at first believed it to be, but, as has gradually become clear, a kind of dialectical process, a dialogue or discussion between two persons." In one of his essays on psychotherapy, he states: "We arrive at the dialectical formulation which tells us precisely that psychic interference is the reciprocal reaction of two psychic systems."

P. W. Martin in his account of the Jungian technique summarizes:

> In a sense, as Jung has pointed out, technique is a somewhat misleading term to apply to the various psycho-perceptive methods used. It suggests a more or less automatic functioning. Actually the constructive technique is in the main a matter of attitude. This is not to suggest that the methods employed are in any sense unimportant. On the contrary, for most people they are indispensable. But unless the basic attitude behind them is right, they will not work.[61]

What then is the right attitude? This, in a sense, is for each person to discover for himself. There is no universally valid prescription. Expressed in general terms, though, I should say that it is an attitude compounded of serious attention, involvement, and objectivity, together with a basic steadfastness of spirit.

A basic fact underlying the function and need of "helpers" at some point in the growth process is that development is the development of an individual and inasmuch as that is so, the development of each individual constitutes a unique way. Paradoxically, the way for an individual being to reach universality is in the fulfillment of his individual nature, just as an artist deepens his vision of an individual form until the whole world seems to speak through it.

Seen from this perspective, everything that has been said in the foregoing pages about the left-hand path, whether in action, feeling, knowing, or physical disciplines, amounts to a stress on individual development; it is the way of stressing the uniqueness of the person and the moment, respecting it as God's will and God's gift, and trusting that this uniqueness, like that of a seed, will gradually unfold the hidden plan and purpose. The alternative style is one that stresses the universal (the law, the symbols or archetypes, the teachings) and expects that such universal nourishment or light will be assimilated or reflected in every individual in a unique way. And here is where the system can either be assimilated or translated into individual terms, or become a deadening formalism that drowns the individual.

The teacher-therapist-guide is the person who, by virtue of his own individual understanding of a system, may help another individual in this process of creative translation of the general into the particular, of the Way into a given, unique way. Each individual is a variation on a universal theme, and a teacher is one with enough insight into the theme to know how the idea may become flesh and deed.

Since the development is that of the individual self, the natural reaction of the undeveloped (most notably in children) is to find his own missing center of judgment and decision in another. This makes the helping relationship one of authority, in which one individual is in some measure giving power to another. It is the ultimate function of the teacher to return his power, guiding the person to find in himself the inner teacher or authority that he is seeking outside. Yet, in practice a guide acts like a temporary "substitute I," so that much of what happens in psychotherapy, for instance, constitutes on the side of the patient a crossing of limits, a going beyond himself, a disrupting of his ordinary patterns of behavior in terms of the demands of the therapist or the rules of the therapeutic relation. By obeying his externalized self (probably closer to his real self than his disturbed personality) the individual thus becomes more receptive to his own self, to his own deeper feelings and motivations which were always in him but to which he would not listen or follow. Before obeying himself, he must learn to obey. His personality has to be broken or made flexible before he can be attuned to his inner voices. In religious terms, these statements are equivalent to the concept that God is always present but we are not ready to give ourselves to Him.

The notion stated above may shed some light on the weight that some Eastern schools give to the strict obedience to a guru.* A guru is somebody who is closer to God than the disciple; therefore obedience to him is the closest approximation to an obedience to God. Thus, we read in Meher Baba:

> Love is a gift from God to man.
> Obedience is a gift from Master to man.
> Surrender is a gift from man to Master.

> One who loves desires the will of the Beloved.
> One who obeys does the will of the Beloved.
> One who surrenders knows nothing but the will
>   of the Beloved.

---

* In many traditions the distinction is drawn between the guru proper, who is a living example of the self-realized man and who teaches by his mere being, and the ordinary teacher, who prescribes techniques and is able to supervise or advise but has not attained his own goal. When this is the case, however, he may become a limiting influence.

Love seeks union with the Beloved.
Obedience seeks the pleasure of the Beloved.
Surrender seeks nothing.

One who loves is the lover of the Beloved.
One who obeys is the beloved of the Beloved.
One who surrenders has no existence other than
    the Beloved.

Greater than love is obedience.
Greater than obedience is surrender.
All three arise out of, and remain contained in,
    the Ocean of divine Love.[62]

It may be interesting to consider here David Bakan's thesis that Freud's interpretation of dreams originated in Freud's acquaintance with a trait in Jewish mysticism much in the spirit of the above quotation. To the Hasidim, the *zaddik* (spiritual guide) was, as in the other traditions, a representative of God, and therefore he was studied by his disciples, every act of his being interpreted for its ultimate significance as a message. What Freud did, according to Bakan,[63] was to democratize the process of interpretation, so that he took the methods applied to the holy texts and to the person of the master, and applied them to every man's soul. In this regard, his was a step toward the left-hand pattern.

Much more could be said of the function of personal relationship as the context for the educational, therapeutic, or spiritual process. For instance, the whole issue may be seen as one in which relationships in general (interpersonal and intrapersonal) are transformed by means of the transformation, healing, or completion being achieved in the form of one given relationship. Such a view may be useful to hold in mind in order not to forget the nonverbal and nonintellectual factors involved in the process. This may be best understood if we think of the legacy of a good mother-child or father-child relationship or a successful therapeutic relationship, and the principle may be as important in the relationship with a spiritual guide. It may be illuminating to consider the following biographic passage from Lama Anagarika B. Govinda concerning his initiation:

> The moment we try to analyse, to conceptualise, or to rationalise the details and experiences of initiation, we are dealing only with dead fragments, but not with the living flow of force, which is expressed in the Tibetan word *dam-ts'hig,* the inner relationship between Guru and Chela and the spontaneous movement, emotion, and realisation on which this relationship is based.
>
> There is nothing secret in the process of initiation, but everybody has to experience it for himself. By trying to explain what goes beyond words we only succeed in dragging the sacred down to the level of the profane, thus losing our own *dam-ts'hig* without benefiting others. By glibly talking about the mystery, we destroy the purity and spontaneity of our inner attitude and the deep reverence which is the key to the temple of revelations. Just as the mystery of love can only unfold when it is withdrawn from the eyes of the crowd, and as a lover will not discuss the beloved with outsiders, in the same way the mystery of the inner transformation can only take place if the secret force of its symbols is hidden from the profane eyes and the idle talk of the world.
>
> What is communicable are only those experiences that belong to the plane of our mundane consciousness, and beyond this we may be able to speak about the results and conclusions to which our experiences have led us. . . .
>
> Among those personalities, Tomo Geshe Rimpoche was undoubtedly the greatest. The inner bond which was created on the day on which I received the *abhiseka,* my first and therefore most important initiation, became a constant source of strength and inspiration. How much the Guru would be able to help me by his

presence, even beyond his death, this I guessed as little in those days as I was conscious of the fact that he was one of the most highly revered religious teachers of Tibet and that for millions of people his name was equated with the highest attainments on the Buddha's spiritual path.[64]

It would seem that just as life proceeds from life, the spark of individuality can only be struck from an accomplished individual, and only an awakened one can wake up a sleeping man. What is the nature of such spiritual influence? It certainly contains an element of learning by subtle imitation, as a musician may learn from a great performer. A great man may radiate something of his spirit in manifestations as subtle as his breathing, gait, or tone of voice, and a true disciple will contact the spirit rather than imitate the outward form. Yet, perhaps the wisest that we can do is leave the question partly open, and not answer with a "nothing but."

What seems clear is that the principle underlying the oral tradition of esotericism, the direct transmission of understanding, is also that of all growth-oriented relationships, including that most elemental one of mothering.* Relationship transcends discrete activities like the passing on of information or the manipulation of one individual by another. In relating there is an interaction between two uniquenesses and a form of learning not divorced from being. When it comes to the goal of development, it seems that no qualification for the one in the helping position is more crucial than the degree of his own personal development—a fact too often forgotten in a fact-oriented education.

* We know from experiments in rats, goats, monkeys, as well as from the observation of humans, that the ability or interest in mothering and of loving in general are in proportion to the quality of the mothering received. Even in rats, where we would tend to think that instinct is all powerful, an animal that was not mothered fails when it is its own turn to tend its litter. And a monkey that has been provided with all satisfactions minus that of contact with an adult during his childhood becomes a "neurotic" adult animal incapable of developing good monkey relationships.

If education as an institution were to profit from the assimilation of resources of other cultures or areas of endeavor that are relevant to its aims, the first step in that assimilation would actually have to be the exposure of teachers to the experience of such resources and ways.

THE ONENESS OF EXPERIENCE
IN THE WAYS OF GROWTH

Cows are of many different colors, but the
Milk of all is of one color, white;
So the proclaimers who proclaim the truth
Use many varying forms to put it in,
But yet the truth enclosed in all is One.
                              —*Upanishads*

Jesus put many cloths of many hues into one
jar, and out of it they came with all their
hues washed off, all clean and white,
As seven colored rays merge in white light.
                              —Sufi text

The purpose of the following pages is to point at what could
be regarded as the experiential meeting ground of the diverse
techniques, exercises, and procedures which are the object of

our inquiry. In the previous chapters we have already encountered their essential unity of concern beyond peripheral associations in the quests for sanity, salvation, and personal growth.
If there is such a convergence of the ultimate ends of psychiatry, religion, and education, we should be able to discern a
similar process in their respective methods, however different
these may appear at first glance.

We have also discussed and classified some of the ways in
terms of their main objective—the will, the higher feelings,
wisdom, and consciousness. By looking at them from the point
of view of the development of such faculties we have reduced
their multiplicity to partial unities. In speaking of the ways of
action, for instance, we have noted three basic approaches that
cut across times and traditions: right action, where the issue is
what is done; right doing, where the emphasis lies upon the
how; and attunement, where the accent is upon the development of a receptivity toward the inner voice of *dharma.* Likewise, in dealing with the ways of feeling, we have encountered
three types of approach, which for practical purposes we might
refer to as the devotional, the cathartic, and the ascetic. In the
domain of knowledge, we have contrasted the attitude in
which there is a predominance of faith (regarded as a temporary acceptance of working ideas) with the other two where reliance upon evidence and experience predominate. In sum, we
have posited a number of fundamental styles in the approach
to human development and education (twelve of them, resulting from the threefold division of each of the four ways of
action, feeling, knowing, and consciousness) which could also
be seen as compatible components, rarely found in pure form.
These styles constitute four clusters which converge upon the
final goal of the complete human being.

The forms of approach followed in the previous chapter,

though, still fail to show the considerable overlap and similarity in details among the basic four. We have stressed the unity among those falling under each of these categories and thus narrowed them down to four, but failed to show the extent of unity across or beyond the four main directions and basic styles. In order to do this, we have to attack the matter of *what* the ways do at a different level.

There are at least three aspects in which we can speak of what a procedure *does*.

To one of these aspects belong most of the expressions used in the foregoing chapters. When we speak of development, healing, salvation, as when we say that a method serves to develop higher feelings, will, or wisdom, we are speaking of *goals*. What the corresponding method *does* is to accomplish these goals.

A second way we might compare what different approaches do is by considering the behavioral, procedural, instrumental, or technical sides of all of them.

Even an external—i.e., "objective"—examination of the approaches mentioned in our research can reveal common elements embedded in their distinctive Gestalt. The training of the ability to summon up and hold vivid images in front of "the mind's eye," for instance, may be found in systems as distinct from one another as the Jewish Kabbalah, the Tantric school of Buddhism, magical traditions, Saint Ignatius's spiritual exercises, and forms of psychotherapy. The focusing of attention on a single object, again, constitutes a link between the exercise of counting the breath in Zen, mantra yoga, sensory awareness, and all the approaches listed above.

If we move from the level of elements or aspects of the ongoing technical procedures to that of the specific processes involved, we can also arrive, by analysis and abstraction, at encompassing notions such as the promotion of self-expression or insight, which also cut across the apparent diversity of some methods.

The present chapter, however, will not deal with either of the above-mentioned regions of commonality—ends, procedures, inferred or observed processes—but with the *experience* elicited by the practice of the different ways. It is with this domain of experiencing that most therapeutic systems and other inward arts are concerned, and it is from the quality of experience that much of their terminology derives. It is in this domain of subjectivity that I will try to show processes that seem to be involved in the different attempts to change man for the better.

In proposing that there are common experiential ingredients in the processes that constitute the psychological reaction to the practice of different systems, I am not implying that there are no differences of emphasis or in individual suitability between these ways. Also, dealing with such experiential common ground from the point of view of different "issues" does not mean that they are basically different, for they overlap and may be understood as aspects of a single change process and facets of a single state. For this very reason the list of aspects with which I am dealing could be thought of as longer or shorter, just as a greater or smaller number of views may be chosen by a photographer to present a three-dimensional sculpture by his two-dimensional medium. Granted this measure of arbitrariness, I will propose that we look at the process of psychological healing-enlightenment-development as one of

(1) shift in identity;

(2) increased contact with reality;

(3) simultaneous increase in both participation and detachment;

(4) simultaneous increase in freedom and the ability to surrender;

(5) unification—intrapersonal, interpersonal, between body and mind, subject and object, Man and God;

(6) increased self-acceptance; and

(7) increase in consciousness.

Some of these terms, like "participation" or "freedom," could be understood in an external or behavioral sense, but this is not the sense intended here. What we will be dealing with, in each instance, is purely subjective reactions, or, better, experiential realities: the *attitude* of freedom, the *inner stance* of participation without which the most frantic action would be that of an automaton; the *state* of surrender, which is possible even in the absence of external pressures.

The expressions in the list above might also be taken to stand for goals, and that would be legitimate: the complete human being may be described as more *himself,* more in contact with reality, more able both to participate and maintain detachment, more free and yet more able to surrender, more accepting of his nature and limitations, and more conscious. These, though, are not only goals, but also what we could regard as inner actions. To surrender to something, to accept an aspect of ourselves, or to become aware of an experience are things that we can "do" more inwardly and subtly than we can move our limbs or vocal cords. These "actions" are, as I expect to show below, *the real actions behind the apparent ones* in the various ways of growth.

Moreover, the various external forms may be understood as a means of lending support to the inner activity and/or monitoring its development; means of making the invisible visible, so that it may be carried out with greater clarity by him who is still unfamiliar with the subtle domain of the central processes. It is as if form was the shadow of the real object, but this shadow is the only visible manifestation of that object available to the beginner. Awareness of mental events, for instance, is subtle and elusive, so that the practice of awareness of the more tangible event of breathing can be helpful in showing what awareness really is. Similarly, some of the widely recognized aspects of a practical life or of a philosophy geared to personal growth (like that of acting without thought of extrinsic rewards or living in the present) may be hard to interpret or come to grasp as more than concepts when not embodied in a practical discipline conducted under supervision. In *aikido,* for instance, the student may discover that any thought of the future, indulgence in fantasy, or looking at himself with the eyes of the audience is likely to result in his being tossed over.

Still, forms and methods run the risk of becoming just forms when the external action becomes an end in itself, and the inner action is forgotten. Regardless of whether the overt task be one of counting the breath, disclosing feelings, dancing or fencing, the individual guided by an authoritative teacher in each of these ways *will be doing the same thing,* putting himself in a certain state, attitude, or form of connection with his being and his action which, being a "state," cannot be properly described but perhaps only expressed. Its expression, indeed, constitutes the content of the highest art.

To say anything *about* this core condition or state of being means tearing it into parts, just as a biologist does in seeking the understanding of life in the dissection of its dead forms. This is what I have done in the sevenfold phenomenological analysis that follows. I hope, though, that the reader may bring together again in his heart what I have artificially separated in the ink.

To assimilate our food into our own substance we must mince it and tear it apart into its basic constituents, and this makes the synthesis possible—the synthesis that we are.

Identity: Experience of Self vs. Self-Image.

The one who knows his self knows God.

—*Saying of* MOHAMMED

By incessantly pursuing within yourself the enquiry, "Who am I?" you will know your true self and thereby attain salvation.

—SRI RAMANA MAHARSHI

The notion of bondage to a self-image as a central aspect in the understanding of personality disorders has loomed large in the history of psychoanalysis. One of the most articulate developments of this notion in the theory of neurosis is presented by Karen Horney in her book *Neurosis and Human Growth.*[1] According to her—stating it briefly—a human being, like a seed, brings into the world some potentialities, but needs for their development certain environmental conditions. These are rarely met, because they depend on parental attitudes, and parents are affected by neuroses that are part of the culture itself. The reaction of the child to surroundings that fall short of meeting his needs is "basic anxiety," the feeling of being in a potentially hostile environment. The reaction to anxiety is that of manipulating the environment to insure security, and this may be done in three ways: by moving against people, fighting for one's needs; by moving toward people, to secure the protection of a powerful provider in symbiotic attachment; or by moving away from people for safety, and finding the maximum resources in one's self. According to conditions and innate predisposition, one of these strategies will be more suitable than the others, and out of a need for consistency it will be chosen as the main ingredient in the style of relating. But in every given situation there will be conflict among the three reaction patterns, and the anxiety behind all three needs will make choice a rigid matter. Then, conflict adds to insecurity. To minimize conflict, reactions other than the dominant one become repressed; the assertive person rejects all feelings and promptings in order to submit, for instance; or the withdrawing type will repress both dominance and dependence. This is experienced as an impoverishment in personality and a restriction of spontaneity. The "solution" is to make up for this impoverishment and insecurity by *idealizing* the dominant solution. So the dominant type idealizes courage, force, directness, etc., repressing everything soft, weak, needful; the meek one feels proud of his gentleness and loving concern for others, regarding all hostility as evil; and the detached type creates, as a support for his behavior, the "virtues" of serenity, reserve, independence, and so on. What was a need has become a virtue, and from now on life consists in living up to these virtues and keeping away from their opposites. What Freud saw as introjection of parental commands and values is for Horney a more autonomous process by which the individual creates his own commands, using or not the parental models. Such a process is a compulsive one: it stems from being cornered by life and ends up in the "tyranny of the should." Whenever the person lives up to his system of shoulds, he feels proud; otherwise self-hate ensues, conscious or not. And self-hate becomes chronic, because the shoulds are impossible to satisfy in their absoluteness. The person's real feelings, thoughts, and urges cannot possibly fit in with the rigid idealization of the self, and they are estranged. The person has truly sold his soul to the devil in order to meet his personal standards of glory—and lost his true self.

A comparable notion of a true self that is covered up by a mask which the person mistakes for his true identity, is found in Jung's concepts of self and persona. I will not go into his proposed polarities of persona vs. shadow, and ego vs. self; it is enough for the present purposes that we consider his notion of persona which is that of a "mask" shown to the world. Jung does not state that it would be desirable to drop such a mask, but, on the contrary, he recognizes that this has protective and adaptive functions which could be compared to those of a healthy skin. What he sees as unnecessary and undesirable is the pervasive *identification* of people with their masks or roles. To the question of "Who am I?" many will probably answer with "a lawyer, a middle-aged, middle-class American," and so on, and as such they will experience themselves in their everyday lives, rather than out of the unlabeled totality of their being. To Jung, the self is not another aspect or fragment of the personality, but only another psychological "center of gravity." A person who identifies with the persona believes part of himself to be his whole psychological reality, whereas one whose consciousness identifies with the core of the self is at the center of his being, *having* his persona and other parts or processes, but *being* his totality. Much the same idea is expressed by the metaphor that we are usually living in only one room of our house. This house is actually a palace, with towers, *salons,* and gardens, but we are locked up in the kitchen or perhaps in the cellar, believing that this is the whole house.

The idea of a shift in identity appears again, in different forms, in Gestalt therapy. Most central to it is the notion that we "disown" aspects of our personality by narrowing the boundaries of the ego. By drawing a boundary between what we call I and not-I in our processes, we give up responsibility, but we also become impoverished. The assumption in Gestalt therapy is that all that "happens" in us *is our doing,* yet it is not the doing of the ego that may be talking at the moment—the particular personality fragment saying "I" in the name of the whole. It is instead the doing of our organism—the interdependent totality of our processes—and to the degree that we take responsibility for it, becoming aware of how *we do* it, we become our organism, our totality. Just as in the Jungian terms, *we become what we already are,* unknowingly.

It is interesting to compare the analytic, Jungian, and Gestalt ways to the self. Analysis proper, whether in psychotherapy or other domains, is a process of taking apart, from which it is expected that reorganization may occur. Just like a sculptor who brings out a form from a rock by taking away what does not belong in it, the analyst is letting the inner man emerge by removing obstacles, or, rather, by letting these melt in the fire of consciousness. In speaking of an emergence of the inner, in this context, I do not necessarily imply expression in action, which is already a consequence, but emergence into consciousness, which amounts to a waking up of the self, a person's knowing himself as he is, rather than believing (or deceiving) himself to be what he "should" be.

Jung's approach to the self is not essentially analytical, in spite of the label of Analytical Psychology borne by his school. As early as 1935 Jung stated: "Silberer distinguishes between the psychoanalytic and the anagogic interpretation, while I distinguish between the analytic-reductive and the synthetic-hermeneutic interpretation." [2]

Jung's strategy is essentially that of illuminating ordinary experience with the light of the mythical, or, to put it more appropriately, letting the mythical light shine forth through the quotidian. Instead of pointing out the inconsequential, the abortive, regressive, and negative aspects of life and dreams, he attempts to show that in every bit of ordinary existence there lie the great laws, the great symbols, the great issues. Thus he underlines the transcendent in the apparently accidental, and facilitates the emergence of the archetypal by nourishing it with its own reflection. If analysis is a removing of obstacles, a killing of the false images of self that obstruct the awareness of self-reality, Jung's approach is that of coaxing the awareness of the self by presenting it with a mirror in the therapist's observations and in the mythical themes which speak of man's core of common experience.

In Gestalt therapy, the main approach to "reassimilating the disowned" is perhaps that of enacting one's involuntary processes. By voluntarily doing what is commonly automatic in us, we establish—or rediscover—a link between the process and us. By acting out a character in a dream, for instance, we may discover that it was a projection (i.e., an illusory other) and contact that core of our experience that was expressing itself indirectly through such otherness. Likewise, in impersonating our voice, or any spontaneous movement—a rocking in the chair, a nod, a smile—by "becoming" them and giving them a voice, we may find that we are only becoming what we already are: somebody *wanting* to do all that, choosing to do so, and finding satisfaction in it, rather than a passive subject of such "occurrences."

In the above discussion I have been viewing the therapeutic process as one in which the alternative to identification with a self-image is the experiencing of the self, a direct contact with one's reality rather than a substitution of a "better" self-image for the old one. I want to elaborate on the contrast between these views, for the latter is at the root of at least one therapeutic system in our survey (Maxwell Maltz's Psychocybernetics[3]) and a concept commonly expressed in less systematic terms.

Maltz's claim is that our self-image (i.e., what we believe we are) is usually not the most conducive to successful living, and that if we can change our self-perception (through autosuggestion) in the direction of greater appreciation, this can have a positive influence on our behavior. The truth of this statement can hardly be debated. Supportive psychotherapy is also based on the assumption that approval leads to greater self-acceptance with repercussions that go far beyond momentary pleasure. What are these repercussions, and how do they affect us? Self-acceptance leads to increased self-expression (less censorship) and self-expression to self-discovery and the tasting of one's identity. One self-image may be more or less conducive to an *openness to experience* than another, just as the belief in man's intrinsic goodness or badness leads to alternative styles in the raising of children and education.

A shift in identity is involved in the change of self-image, but this shift is still not the one that is the outcome of effective psychotherapy, of productive religious pursuit, or of ideal education. Openness to experience that depends on a preconception of the self (however conducive to the experience the self-image may be) still does not make a person free. Such a preconception may be used as a crutch, a device, but still falls short of the aim, which is represented by a condition where openness to experience is unconditional, and constitutes its own reward.

A child growing up in an atmosphere of blame will take on a picture of himself as essentially bad, and under this conviction will never allow himself to look into his reality, which could show him his mistake. Conversely, a child who grows up in an atmosphere of acceptance does not have to hang on to an image of himself according to which he is all right. He feels free to experience himself and be as he is, and in the process he comes to know, moment after moment, whether he is adequate or not. Likewise, a patient in a supportive setting may begin to unfold and discover his reality, which was hidden by his preconception of himself. There will always be a self-image, in the sense of self-perception, but not in the sense of identity. The truly mature person does not need the assurance of being this or that, and having to prove it, mainly because he does not deceive himself into believing that he *is* this or that. The power of our self-image arises, as Horney brilliantly shows, from our belief (mostly unconscious) in our perfection and we are therefore vulnerable to everything in ourselves and others that may contradict our self-idealization.

The opposite of the dependence on an identification with a self-image is the openness to the perception and acceptance of whatever our reality may be at the moment. Our reality at the moment is our *experience*. We cannot know the Kantian "things in themselves," but our experience of ourselves and the world is something that we can either accept (i.e., experience consciously) or reject, repress, disown. In his book *The Politics of Experience*, Ronald D. Laing makes a statement that may be taken as a definition of psychiatry:

> I am a specialist, God help me, in events in inner space and time, in experiences called thoughts, images, reveries, dreams, visions, hallucinations, dreams of memories, memories of dreams, memories of visions, dreams of hallucinations, refractions of refractions of refractions of that original Alpha and Omega of experience and reality, that Reality on whose repression, denial, splitting, projection, falsification, and general desecration and profanation our civilization as much as on anything is based.[4]

When we turn from the psychological literature to that of mysticism we find a similar acknowledgment of a process that entails a shattering of the self-image and the realization of "who we truly are." In the formulation of Vedanta this is expressed as the realization of the self (atman) beyond the limitation of the personal ego (ahankara). In that of Buddhism, it is expressed in the doctrine of non-ego (*Anatta*) that denies ego or separate existence distinct from the *suchness* of all things. In theistic formulations, naturally, the shift in identity is seen as one taking place from the human personality to the Divine Being. As Saint Catherine of Genoa puts it, "My *me* is God: nor do I know my selfhood except in God."

The process of which we are speaking is at the heart of the so-called mystical death and rebirth, in which the outer man ceases to be and the inner man is born. The "death" aspect of it is conveyed by the Buddhistic nirvana (meaning "extinction," and signifying also a transcendence of death); by the Christian "death in Christ," and by the Moslem *fanā-fillah* (extinction into God). The rebirth/awakening aspect is implied in all of these, for nirvana is conceived as mukti (liberation and extinction of individuality in God) which means the recognition that God is what we truly are, while we deceive ourselves into believing that we are our individual masks. Our true being is "Christ in us" (Saint Paul). Every human being is the Buddha, without knowing it. Though the word *rebirth* is true to the quality of the experience, its nature is more that of an awakening to the realization of the nature of the self.

The idea of a change in identity, expressed in terms of rebirth, vanishing of the ego, merging with a deeper self, becoming one with the common identity of all existence or with God, awakening from a dream or understanding our true nature, is so prominent in religious literature that I will only remind the reader of the relevance of this issue.

The difference between the psychological and the religious ways of formulating the self is that for the psychological way, the manifestation of self belongs to an individual entity, whereas the religious view goes beyond. It tells us that whoever truly "sees into his being" (e.g., *kensho,* in Zen) and realizes his identity will find that his self is a drop in an infinite ocean of existence, that he is a microcosm replicating the whole macrocosm, that his soul (atman) is one with the soul of everything (Brahma), that, truly, there is no "self," but only a oneness of everything (which may or may not be called "God") under the illusion of individual existence.

> O pilgrims for the Shrine! Where go ye, where?
> Come back! come back! The Beloved is here!
> His presence all your neighbourhood doth bless!
> Why will ye wander in the wilderness!
> Ye who are seeking God! Yourselves are He!
> Ye need not search! He is ye, verily!
> Why will ye seek for what was never lost?
> There is Naught-Else-than-ye! Be not doubt-tost! [5]
> —SHAMS TABRIZ

> The wise see in their heart the face of God,
> And not in images of stone and clod!
> Who in themselves, alas! can see Him not,
> They seek to find Him in some outer spot! [6]
> —SHIVA PURANA

Alan Watts has throughout his works reformulated these views in terms more familiar to the style of our age. "We suffer from a hallucination, from a false and distorted sensation of our existence as living organisms." As he sums up in *The Book:*

Most of us have the sensation that "I myself" is a separate center of feeling and action, living inside and bounded by the physical body—a center which "confronts" an "external" world of people and things, making contact through the senses with a universe both alien and strange. Everyday figures of speech reflect this illusion. "I came into this world." "You must *face* reality." "The conquest of nature."

This feeling of being lonely and very temporary visitors in the universe is in flat contradiction to everything known about man (and all other living organisms) in the sciences. We do not "come into" this world; we come *out* of it, as leaves from a tree. As the ocean "waves," the universe "peoples." Every individual is an expression of the whole realm of nature, a unique action of the total universe. This fact is rarely, if ever, experienced by most individuals. Even those who know it to be true in theory do not sense or feel it, but continue to be aware of themselves as isolated "egos" inside bags of skin.

The first result of this illusion is that our attitude to the world "outside" us is largely hostile. We are forever "conquering" nature, space, mountains, deserts, bacteria, and insects instead of learning to cooperate with them in a harmonious order.[7]

Statements like Watts's make the mystical view understandable to us not merely as the outcome of a special subjective state, but as stemming from a grasp of objective reality. However this may be, we must not forget that both religious and psychiatric ideas are not so much the outcome of speculation as the formulation of experiences. The notion of self in psychological writing reflects the *experience* of self in persons who have undergone the therapeutic process, just as the religious conception of the self is the reflection of the mystical experience.

The question that poses itself is whether these two experiences—that of healing and that of mystical union—are different in the sense of belonging to separate domains of experience, or are just different stages in a single change-process. If the latter were true, we might conceive that the experience of psychological integration—the finding of the real self—might be a preliminary step before entering the domain of mystical experience, crowned by the realization that Christianity expresses as "I and my Father are one." Perhaps we still need time to obtain the final answer in this matter, but there seems to be a growing trend of opinion toward this last alternative. Contemporary psychotherapy sees more and more the relevance of the Eastern disciplines, and many of its outstanding representatives share the belief that they may be speaking of the more advanced steps in man's jungle path of evolution. Jung, for instance, writes in his comments to *The Tibetan Book of the Dead:*

The only "initiation process" that is still alive and practiced today in the West is the analysis of the unconscious as used by doctors for therapeutic purposes. This penetration into the ground-layers of consciousness is a kind of rational maieutics in the Socratic sense, a bringing forth of psychic contents that are still germinal, subliminal, and as yet unborn. Originally, this therapy took the form of Freudian psychoanalysis and was mainly concerned with sexual fantasies. This is the realm that corresponds to the last and lowest region of the *Bardo,* known as the *Sidpa Bardo,* where the dead man, unable to profit by the teachings of the Chih-kai and *Chönyid Bardo,* begins to fall a prey to sexual fantasies and is attracted by the vision of mating couples. Eventually he is caught by a womb and born into the earthly world again. Meanwhile, as one might expect, the Oedipus complex begins to function. If his karma destines him to be reborn as a man, he will fall in love with his mother-to-be and will find his father hateful and disgusting. Conversely, the future daughter will be highly attracted by her father-to-be and repelled by her mother. The European passes through this specifically Freudian domain when his unconscious contents are brought to light under analysis, but he goes in the reverse direction. He journeys back through the world of infantile-sexual fantasy to the womb. It has even been suggested in psychoanalytical circles that the trauma par excellence is the birth-experience itself—nay more, psychoanalysts even claim to have probed back to memories of intra-uterine origin. Here Western reason reaches its limit, unfortunately. I say "unfortunately" because one rather wishes that Freudian psychoanalysis could have happily pursued these so-called intra-uterine experiences still further back; had it succeeded in this bold undertaking, it would surely have come out beyond the *Sidpa Bardo* and penetrated from behind into the lower reaches of the *Chönyid Bardo.*

And further on:

Freudian psychoanalysis, in all essential aspects, never went beyond the experiences of the *Sidpa Bardo;* that is, it was unable to extricate itself from sexual fantasies and similar "incompatible" tendencies which cause anxiety and other affective states. Nevertheless, Freud's theory is the first attempt made by the West to investigate, as if from below, from the animal sphere of instinct, the psychic territory that corresponds in Tantric Lamaism to the *Sidpa Bardo.* A very justifiable fear of metaphysics prevented Freud from penetrating into the sphere of the "occult." In addition to this, the *Sidpa* state, if we are to accept the psychology of the *Sidpa Bardo,* is characterized by the fierce wind of karma, which whirls the dead man along until he comes to the "womb-door." In other words, the *Sidpa* state permits of no going back, because it is sealed off against the *Chönyid* state by an intense striving downwards, towards the animal sphere of instinct and physical rebirth. That is to say, anyone who penetrates into the unconscious with purely biological assumptions will become stuck in the instinctual sphere and be unable to advance beyond it, for he will be pulled back again and again into physical existence. It is therefore not possible for Freudian theory to reach anything except an essentially negative valuation of the unconscious. It is a "nothing but." At the same time, it must be admitted that this view of the psyche is typically Western, only it is expressed more blatantly, more plainly, and more ruthlessly than others would have dared to express it, though at bottom they think no differently. As to what "mind" means in this connection, we can only cherish the hope that it will carry conviction. But, as even Max Scheler noted with regret, the power of this "mind" is, to say the least of it, doubtful.

I think, then, we can state it as a fact that with the aid of psychoanalysis the rationalizing mind of the West has pushed forward into what one might call the neuroticism of the *Sidpa* state, and has there been brought to an inevitable standstill by the uncritical assumption that everything psychological is subjective and personal. Even so, this advance has been a great gain, inasmuch as it has enabled us to take one more step behind our conscious lives. This knowledge also gives us a hint of how we ought to read the *Bardo Thödol*—that is, backwards. If, with the help of our Western science, we have to some extent succeeded in understanding the psychological character of the *Sidpa Bardo*, our next task is to see if we can make anything of the preceding *Chönyid Bardo*.[8]

Aside from an understanding of commonality that may arise from the refining of psychological notions about the change-process, we also have other information to consider which is having great impact on our understanding of the nature of mental health.

Abraham Maslow's investigations of peak-experiences, for instance, indicate that psychologically healthy persons are more prone to report such experiences (formulated or not in religious terms) either because they are more ready to accept them or to become aware of them. We may rephrase this statement by saying that healthy persons are ready to experience states which go beyond our current concept of health as a mere well-functioning system. A characteristic of peak-experiences that is relevant to our discussion here, is the dissolution of boundaries between subject and object, self and not self.

Dr. Stanislaus Grof's group in Czechoslovakia has presented challenging information as to what happens when psychedelic therapy is carried beyond the moment when the change-process satisfies the ordinary standards of mental health. He has presented the only available data on the outcome of prolonged administration of LSD-25 in large doses within the context of psychotherapy. His subjects fell into three groups, according to their initial psychological condition: psychotics, neurotics, and "normals" (the last group consisted of members of the medical and premedical staff at the hospital in which the research was conducted). Briefly stated, the main observations in the course of 60–90 weekly sessions were as follows:

(1) The psychotic group improved over a period of months to the point of apparent normalcy and then started exhibiting symptoms of increasing severity, until there was a relapse of psychotic manifestations. The character of this second psychotic bout was different from the first in some respects, and some individuals were able to emerge from it completely cured after an experience described as a "rebirth."

(2) Psychoneurotics differed from psychotics in that the duration of their period of initial improvement was shorter, and their relapse therefore came about sooner. After continuation of their sessions, some evinced transient psychotic manifestations but most did not. After the final crisis, a large percentage of them were considered to be completely cured.

(3) "Normals" reported gains from the sessions after a very short period of time and arrived at the critical stage much faster than either one of the other two groups.

Dr. Grof's background was Freudian, but his categories of analysis had to change to deal with the types of experience reported by his subjects at different stages in their treatment; after the first weeks Rankian concepts became more appropriate, and later still those of Jungian psychology seemed to fit. Finally, his patients entered a domain of experience which only the language and symbolism of mystical traditions could express.[9]

Regardless of whether we prefer the secular or the religious formulation of the self—whether or not we see mystical overtones in the nature of our experience of ourselves when liberated from our fears and preconceptions—let us now try to understand some instances of ways of growth in terms of the identity shift that we are discussing.

In considering methods, we need not necessarily do so in terms of the most readily available interpretations of them by the traditions or psychological schools employing them—for when we deal with life and not with mere concepts we may safely assume that any fragment of it can be understood in many alternative ways and from different points of view. At any rate, our concern here is with what a method *does* to a person in terms of the point of view singled out rather than with what it is said to do.

Disciplines explicitly aiming at the dissolution or at a lowering of the ego to its proper place in the functioning of the total personality are numerous among the traditional spiritual disciplines, though apparently very different from one another. Some may appear (especially to those who forget or are unfamiliar with the original meaning of the practice) like moral injunctions. An example is the Christian practice of humility—an antidote to the ego's proud attachment to itself. Others may appear to be life styles required of the religious profession—such as the vows of poverty, chastity, and obedience—all of which are of little consequence if not considered as an attempt at renunciation for the sake of self-image. Even a purely physical discipline, such as a particular craft or sport, may be approached from the point of view of a shift in perceived identity (from ego to self) if practiced by somebody who has the understanding required to apply it. An example may be seen in the following passage from a Japanese master of archery:

> In archery a man must die to his purer nature, the one which is free from all artificiality and deliberation, if he is to reach perfect

enjoyment of Tao. He must learn how to control the emittance of truth, flowing like an eternal spring. Finally, he must be able to reveal Tao in his own attitude on the basis of true "insight." This way is a very easy and direct one. The most difficult thing is to let oneself die completely in the very act of shooting.[10]

More pertinent than any of the practices mentioned this far, though, is the spiritual exercise *par excellence,* which we find, in different forms, in all traditions: *meditation.*

Most types of meditation involve a twofold effort: (1) the cultivation of an "inner silence" or temporary stopping of ego-controlled activities (mainly categorizing and judging) and (2) the attainment of a state of receptivity to aspects of reality that might be called subtle in that they do not fit with pre-established categories. Both "movements" of the mind allow the ego to step out of the way so that selfhood may be manifested and the organism's activity contacted *from within.*

Some forms of meditation may seem utterly simple from their description, and their difficulties and implications only known from experience. One of them, practiced mostly in Buddhistic countries, is what might potentially become an attitude toward everyday experience in general: the practice of watching the stream of consciousness without interfering with its flow.

From our present point of view, it would be called a practice of egoless self-awareness.

> . . . it is the ability to retain one's normal and everyday consciousness and at the same time to let go of it. That is to say, one begins to take an objective view of the stream of thoughts, impressions, feelings and experiences which constantly flows through the mind. Instead of trying to control and interfere with it, one simply lets it flow as it pleases. But whereas consciousness normally lets itself be carried away by the flow, in this case the important thing is to *watch* the flow without being carried away.

In the Chinese metaphysical tradition this is termed *wu-hsin* or "idealessness," signifying a state of consciousness in which one simply accepts experiences as they come without interfering with them on the one hand or identifying oneself with them on the other. One does not judge them, form theories about them, try to control them or attempt to change their nature in any way; one lets them be free to be just exactly what they are.[11]

Other approaches in meditation may be understood from a similar point of view. Let us take a look at za-zen, for instance, where the task is one of non-doing rather than of mindfulness.

"Most of you are beginners, so it may be rather difficult for you to understand why we practice za-zen or meditation in this way," said Shrinyu Suzuki Roshi at a Sesshin in San Francisco in 1966. "We always say, 'just sit,' and if you do, you will find that Zen practice—just to sit—is not easy. Just to sit may be the most difficult thing. To work on something is not difficult; but not to work on anything is rather difficult." [12]

In trying not to do anything, the first thing that the meditator will probably have to "do" is to stop trying. The issue will take him into paradoxical situations: thinking is a deviation from the assignment of non-doing, but so is any attempt to prevent the arising of thoughts. The way out, again, is not anything that he can "do," but rather it is in the nature of a *realization,* a shift in point of view. It lies in the discovery that from the very beginning he has not done anything, and there is nothing he can do, however much he tries, because he is truly a field of consciousness in which processes take place. Thoughts occur, feelings arise, things happen, but the self is like a space in which they take place, unimpeded. As Chuang Tzu puts it, "The perfect man employs his mind as a mirror; it grasps nothing, it refuses nothing, it receives but it does not keep."

The everyday ego that *does* is only an illusion; an illusion of separateness clinging to an illusion of doing, where there is only the universal flow of cause-effect in events. If there is such a thing as a *self*—as a *me*, or *you*—it is either the stream of events itself (which cannot do but just is) or something more like a no-thingness in which it flows. As the Zen patriarch Hui-neng expresses it in his famous sutra:

> Learned Audience, the illimitable Void of the universe is capable of holding myriads of things of various shape and form, such as the sun, the moon, stars, mountains, rivers, worlds, springs, rivulets, bushes, woods, good men, bad men, Dharmas pertaining to goodness or badness, Deva planes, hells, great oceans, and all the mountains of the Mahameru. Space takes in all these, and so does the voidness of our nature. We say that the Essence of Mind is great because it embraces all things, since all things are within our nature. When we see the goodness or the badness of other people we are not attracted by it, nor repelled by it, nor attached to it; so that our attitude of mind is as void as space. In this way, we say our mind is great. Therefore we call it "Maha." [13]

The same that has been said of the above forms of meditation may be seen in many, if not all, others. For instance, everything in the nature of an attempt to "control" the mind will lead to the realization that "I" cannot do so. Only "it" controls itself. *To control "it" I must stop being my "little ego" and become "it," become one with my organismic process, my self-regulated self.*

A more contemporary process is that of *free association* originally introduced by Freud in his clinical practice as an exploratory technique. Throughout the history of psychoanalysis more importance has been given to the therapist's interpretations than to the patient's activity in the analytical process.

Actually, the process of free association is not very different from that of meditation, in that it entails constant watchfulness on one's stream of mental events. One of the differences, naturally, is that it involves the translation of awareness into words, and a certain stress on the conceptual and imagining domains of mental activity. In order to look at free association from a point of view different from the traditional one, I suggest that we first look at some practices that may at first glance seem quite unrelated.

There is an exercise practiced in Asian countries which consists of watching the breath without interfering with its natural rhythm. This is easy to say, but not to do. When unaware of breathing, our metencephalic centers manage to regulate its flow with great natural wisdom. But as soon as we pay attention to it, we also take control. Our ego cannot just watch and let be. It has to *do* everything. The exercise is naturally one of letting the animal in us express itself in full awareness, so that we can at the same time be spontaneous and self-conscious.

We are familiar with the challenge of this situation in our experience of movement. We can either be spontaneous "behind our backs," so to say, as in ordinary walking, writing, laughing, or self-consciously unspontaneous, a state in which *I* am watching, my natural being recoils and my behavior depends on my conscious programing rather than on the richness of my organismic integration. The situation is particularly well known to students of musical instruments who frequently find that their expressiveness diminishes during periods of intensive dedication to the technicalities, such as fingering, skips, tension or relaxation, and so on. Even more than musicians, actors are aware of the need to integrate the spontaneous and the technical, there being schools of acting that emphasize one or the other extreme.

The domain of movement taken as a challenge to be one's

self and yet aware has been cultivated most systematically in the Japanese art of archery and in Zen painting and calligraphy. Eugen Herrigel, in his *Zen in the Art of Archery*[14] describes his own training process in Japan and tells how there came a moment when the experience of "I shoot" switched to that of "it shoots." In other words, it was not his conscious and rational calculating ego that was controlling the process; another kind of functioning was taking place that allowed for a more integrated participation of his faculties. Before achieving this, in doubt and despair he had asked his Master what the "it" was that was meant to shoot the arrow; the teacher replied that when he could know that he would be a Master himself. The change-process in this case consisted in the "he" becoming "it"—the identity of the doer shifting from ego to self.

After looking at the breathing exercise and its counterpart in the medium of movement, we may take a further step, away from the body, and consider what the equivalent of this exercise would be in the domain of thinking. It would amount to *watching the thought-process without interfering with it,* which is precisely the process of *free* association. I stress the word *free* because so-called free association in actual fact is rarely successful. Moreover, much of the analytical process consists in the interpretation of resistance to free association. I think that one of the fundamental statements in the history of psychoanalysis is Ferenczi's remark that the ability to free-associate may be considered a criterion for termination of analysis. The parallel with the case of Zen archery is quite clear. The psychoanalytic patient is required to do, as a means for his cure, what he cannot possibly do. And this request is in essence that he stop doing, that he get out of his own way. To achieve it is in a way to stop being; to stop being the manipulator of his thoughts, and open up to the thinking process as it proceeds when he does not direct it. Experience shows that the outcome is not chaos, but quite the contrary. Not even our dreams are chaotic, and they occur when our ego is asleep. The self has its structure and style, just like our physical organs, our hands, or our noses, but we do not usually trust it, and we introduce an artificial order that stems from our self-image and its concerns; we think what and how we believe we *should* think. In letting go of the self-image, letting it die in us, our true thinking is born.

Free association is to thinking and psychoanalytic form what guided reverie is to the imagination. There, again, the issue is to creatively let the dream unfold and yet be awake in it. We may discern the same process in improvisational theater and in Subud. The *latihan,* derived from dervish tradition, is the least structured of all the practices, and that may account for its potential intensity. It constitutes an attempt to fulfill a surrender to God's will to the person's best understanding of it. It amounts therefore to emptying the mind of preconceptions, shoulds, and restraints; letting go of attempts at controlling one's behavior; and being open to the emergence of the unknown—what *it* wills. In the process, "I" becomes "it," or momentarily disappears to let "it" be.

The use of psychedelic substances provides another way of affecting one's experience of the self. Early in the experimentation with these substances, the users described the occurrence of death-rebirth experiences resembling those in mystic literature, and the term *egoless* has become standard in the description of reactions to LSD. It would seem that different drugs may temporarily suppress one or more aspects of the controlling and censoring mechanisms to which our ordinary sense of identity is linked, so that the person may experience his reality beyond the ordinary self-concept. Interestingly, the resulting experience of the self "when the doors of perception are cleansed" easily leads to the experience of oneness with other beings or forms of life, and this in turn to the mystical realm.

The notions discussed in this section—that of a self to be experienced and that of a self-image or self-concept that must die in the change-process—are more or less familiar to the practitioners of any of the disciplines discussed thus far. If such notions are adequate to explain the unitary process of change, though, they should also be suitable as a model for what happens in a system not inspired by them.

One of the approaches that is most remote from these concepts is behavior therapy. The behavior therapist is concerned with the treatment of symptoms, and to him *the symptoms are the disease.* Symptoms arise from associations established (in the individual's past history) between certain stimuli or situations and pain, anxiety, or discomfort, so that every time the said situation is met it gives rise to one of these undesirable responses. The task of the therapist is therefore to dissociate a given stimulus from the patient's undesirable response. He accomplishes this task by means of deconditioning or reconditioning: he presents the patient with the unpleasant stimulus or situation in increasing degrees of intensity while at the same time presenting him with something pleasurable that may compete with the anxiety or pain being elicited. Experience tells us that after repeated presentations the avoided stimulus will arouse less and less anxiety, until eventually the patient's reaction becomes normal.

If the scope of behavior therapy were just that of curing isolated symptoms, it would hardly deserve to be placed next to systems whose goal is a transformation of personality. Yet, the dimensions of the unit that we can call symptom may vary within wide limits, as well as the nature of the stimulus. Thus, the same general idea that may be applied to the treatment of a fear of open spaces or water may be also applied to a fear of authoritarian figures, of women, or of sexual arousal.

The stimulus in the latter instance is not external but internal: the person's perception of his own motivation (e.g., anger) or physical state (e.g., sexual arousal), which has been linked in his past experience with fear of guilt. Whenever the stimulus that elicits the symptom is an internal process of the individual—behavioral, visceral, mental—rather than an object in the external world, the issue of therapy is equivalent to that of personality transformation. When the behavioral therapist is dealing with this area, though, where the symptom is aroused by certain types of motivation—fantasy, feeling, or thinking that have become "taboo"—he is exactly in that same domain that is characterized by a restriction imposed on experiencing by a set of "shoulds" or inner commands.

In fact, we may broaden the conception of symptom to its limit by speaking of a "fear to be one's self," and deal with this situation directly in the context of conditioning, rewarding self-expression, and punishing deviation from it. The behavioristic and the psychodynamic formulations of neurosis, when they come to the more encompassing levels of symptomatology, are linked by the notion of conditioned anxiety and the internalized prohibition that is at the core of all defenses. I have elsewhere suggested that just as we may understand a repression in terms of conditioning, we may interpret the avoidance response of a rat in a conditioning experiment as an "internalization" of his environment.

But let us now turn to the actual practice of behavior therapy and see how we may understand its effectiveness in terms of its bearing on the self-image. The self-concept regulates all avoidances. Whatever does not match the ego's requirements becomes a threat to its definition of itself. This is why certain experiences (like anger, typically) and the situations that give rise to them come to be feared: they are experienced by the self-image-attached ego as a threat to its very identity, to its very existence. Their catastrophic connotations bespeak death to the ego as it perceives itself. In other words, the person feels as if he were to die because he believes himself to be his self-image (a product of his fantasy) rather than being in touch with his own experience.

What happens as an avoided situation is experienced again with increasing directness in the context of treatment—in the favorable situation provided by the therapist's reassurances, in a state of relaxation, and probably with additional rewards. The behavior therapist assumes that when the situation that elicits the symptom becomes associated with the rewards presented by the therapist, a new conditioned response is being established. Yet it seems unlikely that a new conditioned response strong enough to replace the old one could arise from such mild positive reinforcements as a state of relaxation or the therapist's approval. Let us instead propose the following alternative interpretation: the rewards supplied by the therapeutic context do not become part of a new conditioned response, but are just enough to counteract *for the moment* the confrontation of the unpleasantness aroused by the symptom-arousing stimulus. The value of such neutralization, or support, that then leads the patient to confront the avoided, is that in the process of such confrontation the patient *learns* that his fear was groundless. Anxieties are generally perpetuated by avoiding the situation that originated them, and thus the person misses the opportunity to learn that there is nothing to fear. What is really important is that the person be able to *confront* the situation. In the terms of learning theory, what happens then is the *extinction* of a conditioned response, not the building up of a new one. And, in more general terms, the patient is acquiring more openness to experience—unconditioned responses—in the process of extinction of his past conditionings. To the extent that his conditioning has been at the level of the self-image, he is not merely changing his self-image, but becoming free of one, as his responses are relevant to the present qualities of the situation rather than to fantasies or predictions stemming from the past. In making these statements I am implying that the process of change is not just one of altered programing of behavior or feelings, but one of greater freedom from programed responses, i.e., greater creative choice.

Whether this interpretation is correct or not, I think it is appropriate at this point to consider that behavior therapy and meditation—two approaches of widely divergent backgrounds—are quite similar when considered from the point of view of the experience of the person exposed to the practices. Their common feature is that the *reward* is represented by a state of rest and relaxation, and it is against this background that the patient evokes anxiety-eliciting situations in fantasy. In many forms of meditation the body is kept in a state of relaxation, and when the mind is allowed to wander, it naturally leads to the unresolved conflict-laden areas that press for attention. Thus, what happens in the course of time is that fantasies and reminiscences are contemplated in a state of lucidity, and the person's reaction toward them undergoes a change.

Reality vs. Illusion

The essence of Nirvana consists simply in the extinction of the constructive activity of our imagination.[15]

—CHANDRAKIRTI

Sin being generally conceived as rebellion against the
majesty of God, we have now to inquire after the source or
instigator of this rebellion. In Rabbinic literature this
influence is termed Yezer Hara. This is usually translated
"evil imagination" . . .[16]

—SOLOMON SCHECHTER

The process of human growth that in the foregoing pages we
saw as one of shift in identity may also be viewed, from a different perspective, as one of increased contact with reality.

If we look into the most acute forms of mental disease, there
can hardly be any question as to the delusional quality of its
manifestations. In the spheres of thinking and perception the
psychotic patient displays a feeble grasp of reality. Delusional
thinking, by no means exclusively psychotic, is also a part of
neurotic symptoms or characterologic patterns. In neuroses,
though, it is less obvious as it is implicit in feelings or behavior
rather than explicit in the form of thought disturbances. Freud
has spoken of neurosis as an anachronism, in the sense that the
individual responds to his environment in a way that was once
adequate (in his childhood) but has ceased to be realistic.
Many of our perceptions of the events around us are anachro-
nistic in this sense. Our appreciations, expectations, and fantasies concerning others are not quite realistic, but tinged by
childish views that have become fixed in us. In fact all neurotic
behavior may be interpreted as stemming from a mispercep-
tion of reality, a reality wrapped in superimposed illusory
threats. This is because in a neurosis, as distinct from a psychosis, the individual has two alternate views of the world: one delusional, which is unconscious and controls behavior; and the
other more or less realistic, which is conscious but dissociated
from action and motivation—"the heart has reasons that reason knows not." These hidden and pervasive distortions in the

perception of the world that occur in emotional disturbance are acknowledged throughout psychotherapeutic literature, as in Horney's "unrealistic demands," in Ellis's "wrong propositions," and in the notion of "reality testing" as one of the attributes of mental health, a frequent item in the writing of ego psychologists. It must be noted, though, that the notion of reality testing not only bespeaks the recognition of accurate perception as one of the characteristics of sanity; it has also often been used by psychoanalysts with overtones of "adjustment" to a "consensual reality" that in the eyes of some thinkers (like Fromm or Szasz) is only shared delusion. The latter view is illustrated by a fable from Kahlil Gibran's *The Madman:*

> Once there ruled in the distant city of Wirani a king who was both mighty and wise. And he was feared for his might and loved for his wisdom.
>
> Now, in the heart of that city was a well, whose water was cool and crystalline, from which all the inhabitants drank, even the king and his courtiers; for there was no other well.
>
> One night when all were asleep, a witch entered the city, and poured seven drops of strange liquid into the well, and said, "From this hour he who drinks this water shall become mad."
>
> Next morning all the inhabitants, save the king and his lord chamberlain, drank from the well and became mad, even as the witch had foretold.
>
> And during that day the people in the narrow streets and in the market places did naught but whisper to one another, "The king is mad. Our king and his lord chamberlain have lost their reason. Surely we cannot be ruled by a mad king. We must dethrone him."
>
> That evening the king ordered a golden goblet to be filled from the well. And when it was brought to him he drank deeply, and gave it to his lord chamberlain to drink.
>
> And there was great rejoicing in that distant city of Wirani, because its king and its lord chamberlain had regained their reason.[17]

There is really no contradiction in the statement that mental disease is delusional and that our standards of normality are too. Normality is after all a statistical concept denoting the most frequent, and few would argue today about the psychopathological quality of the modal personality in our culture. So we may retain the notion that mental health is characterized by the perception of reality, while accepting that the ordinary human condition is somewhere in between the extremes of delusion and perception of the truth. This intermediate condition is not characterized so much by the suffering of the individual as by the social aberrations that result from his misperceptions. For this reason Fromm prefers to speak of "socially patterned defects" rather than neurosis. The dogmatic assertions of "truth" and "reality" by different groups sharing different notions of them is central to all prejudice, as the authors of *The Authoritarian Personality*[18] point out and as Eric Hoffer describes in *The True Believer*.[19]

If we now turn from psychotherapy to mysticism, we find that here too reality is a major concern. To Evelyn Underhill, "Mysticism is the art of union with Reality." Naturally, this point of view also stems from the recognition that our "ordinary reality" is to a large extent a mental construct rather than a contact with the world:

> It is notorious that the operations of the average human consciousness unite the self, not with things as they really are, but with images, notions, aspects of things. The verb "to be," which he uses so lightly, does not truly apply to any of the objects amongst which the practical man supposes himself to dwell. For him the hare of Reality is always ready-jugged: he conceives not the living, lovely, wild, swift-moving creature which has been sacrificed in order that he may be fed on the deplorable dish he calls "things as they

really are." So complete, indeed, is the separation of his consciousness from the facts of being, that he feels no sense of loss. He is
happy enough "understanding," garnishing, assimilating the car-
cass from which the principle of life and growth has been ejected,
and whereof only the most digestible portions have been retained.
He is not "mystical."

Furthermore:

> Because mystery is horrible to us, we have agreed for the most part
> to live in a world of labels; to make of them the current coin of ex-
> perience, and ignore their merely symbolic character, the infinite
> gradation of values which they misrepresent. We simply do not at-
> tempt to unite with Reality. But now and then that symbolic
> character is suddenly brought home to us. Some great emotion,
> some devastating visitation of beauty, love, or pain, lifts us to an-
> other level of consciousness; and we are aware for a moment of the
> difference between the neat collection of discrete objects and expe-
> riences which we call the world, and the height, the depth, the
> breadth of that living, growing, changing Fact, of which thought,
> life, and energy are parts, and in which we "live and move and
> have our being." Then we realise that our whole life is enmeshed
> in great and living forces; terrible because unknown.[20]

The stress of mysticism (and esotericism) on reality goes
hand in hand with its concern with contemplation, self-knowledge, and the development of attention and consciousness.
The expression "objective consciousness" used by Gurdjieff,
and the more widespread term "cosmic consciousness" too
stress reality. Objectivity here is not used the way it is used in
science, but more in the Sartrean sense of an apprehension of
reality free from the labels that our mind places, separating us
from our experiences.

The opposite of reality, in the terms of mysticism, is the
world of illusion, which is also that of our ordinary state of

consciousness. It is the *māyā* of the Hindus that leads to attachment, or the "vanity of vanities," or the shadow of reality that
in Plato's myth of the cave man sees, chained with his back to
the real objects.

Enlightenment is a state of knowing and a dissipation of
illusion, so that a Zen monk could say of his *satori*, "At a single
stroke I have completely crushed the cave of phantoms."

We might be tempted to think of a gradient of reality ranging in a line from the delusional extreme of psychosis through
unconscious delusions of neurosis and our standards of normality into the area of peak-experience proneness and mystical
enlightenment. Considering the matter more closely, though,
we might find a circular graph more apt, for there are many
ways in which the extremes of psychosis and enlightenment,
though opposite, lie close to each other.

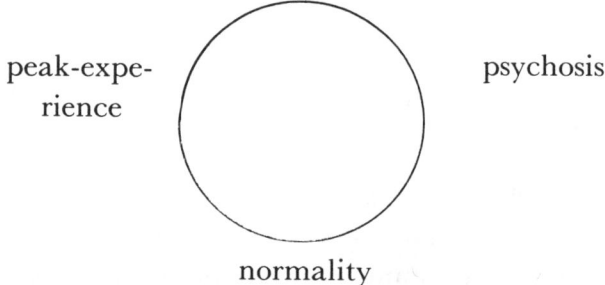

peak-expe-
rience

psychosis

normality

The resemblance between genius and madness has been
noted from old, and it is the similarity-within-the-difference
that led Ernst Kris to posit the notion of "regression in the
service of the ego." [21] According to this, the creative person
would be in command of his surrender, able to relinquish his
defense mechanisms at will.

The point of contact between supernormal and subnormal
forms of the abnormal may be provided by the notion of open-

ness to experience, a concept linking our discussion of identity with that of grasp on reality. Studies on openness to experience (such as Frank Barron's on complexity[22] and Ronald Taft's on ego-permissiveness)[23] suggest that in our "normal state" our range of experience is limited and substituted by an inferential contact with the world, just as our self-identity is substituted for our conceptual, mnemonic self-image.

We might say that normality is pseudo-objectivity. While the psychotic acts out his dreams, we largely relegate our truest affective experience to the unconscious and live in a standardized world of reason; our world view is a system of fairly accurate predictions on our environment. We must realize that this is only a cognitive map, after all; it is not objective experience. Such a map covers up our pathology; a layer of accurate fantasy covers our deeper layer of inaccurate fantasy, which only manifests itself as symptoms, unwarranted moods, dreams. That normality is sometimes compensated or dissimulated psychosis may be shown most convincingly through the artificial suppression of ego functions with psychopharmacological agents. The creative person, in allowing himself to be open to experience to a larger extent than the average person, opens up, too, to the pathology that ordinarily lies buried under a layer of adaptation. He is therefore more anxious than the average person, and he also sees himself as more fulfilled and enjoying moments of great meaningfulness. *The normal situation, then, is like a delusion of nondelusion;* one in which much distorted experience is not taken into account in the dealings with reality. Such dealings, therefore, do not stem from the total personality, but from the masklike censor with which the person identifies, as we discussed in connection with the issue of the self-image.

To say that normality is only the masking of psychotic experience is most probably an overstatement. It is more likely that such a state of compensation is only possible whenever there is no great dissonance between conscious ego perception of reality and unconscious experience. Whenever the discrepancy between them is too large (much reality distortion being present in the experiential side), the gap cannot be bypassed any more and leads to symptoms. Thus the "normal" person may be at the same time more removed from experience than the super- or subnormal in the psychopathological scale, and yet be in between the two extremes in terms of distortion of experience.

The notion that the average condition of humanity is like an inaccurate model of reality covered up by an accurate model has significant implications for our understanding of the ways of growth. Our essential disunity is due to the fact that we interpret the world on two levels (rational vs. irrational, adult vs. child, conscious vs. unconscious, etc.), and our experience cannot change unless we allow ourselves to experience this dichotomy. For healing to take place, the wound must be exposed; for purification to occur, sin is necessary; for growth, immaturity; for totality, nothingness. The way is typically that of a descent into hell, of falling in order to rise, of *reculer pour mieux sauter*. All this entails a willingness to accept the discomfort resulting from giving up temporary adaptation in the *as if* modality of functioning. It is a process of "positive disintegration," as K. Dabrowski puts it; [24] a gradual letting go of the ego's censorships of perception and impulse, which may even lead through psychotic manifestations.

The risk of psychosis has been recognized in the mystical and esoteric ways, and was particularly stressed by Jung as a possible accident in what he called the process of individuation. Later, Maslow spoke of the dangers of B-cognition. Psychotic manifestations are also not infrequent in the terminal stages of successful psychoanalysis. But only recently do we begin to see real recognition of the value of psychotic experience and perhaps the need for it as a stage in the process of deep unification and self-realization. Laing has presented this view most articulately,[25] and Julian Silverman has posited that the initiatory process in shamanism which leads to the fulfillment of an extraordinary personality is essentially that of a psychosis allowed to take its self-healing course.[26]

We may wonder whether the cataclysmic "positive disintegration" of a shaman, a saint, or an enlightened Ramakrishna may be nothing but a stylistic alternative to the long-term activity of a great artist. It is conceivable that just as the former plunge into this depth, with complete surrender of themselves and forgetfulness of external concerns, the successful artist may sometimes be able to receive the shock in small installments, treading more slowly in the midst of long-termed anxiety. That the end may be the same is more than suggested by the following passages of Dante in the last canto of his *Paradiso*:

> For now my sight, clear and yet clearer grown,
>   Pierced through the ray of that exalted light,
>   Wherein, as in itself, the truth is known.
>
> Henceforth my vision mounted to a height
>   Where speech is vanquished and must lag behind,
>   And memory surrenders in such plight.
>
> As from a dream one may awake to find
>   Its passion yet imprinted on the heart,
>   Although all else is cancelled from the mind,
>
> So of my vision now but little part
>   Remains, yet in my inmost soul I know
>   The sweet instilling which it did impart.[27]

or in the following remarks by Beethoven quoted by Bettina von Armin Brentano:

> When I open my eyes I must sigh, for what I see is contrary to my religion, and I must despise the world which does not know that

music is a higher revelation than all wisdom and philosophy, the wine which inspires one to new generative processes, and I am the Bacchus who presses out this glorious wine for mankind and makes them spiritually drunken. When they are again become sober, they have drawn from the sea all that they brought with them, all that they can bring with them to dry land. I have not a single friend, I must live alone. But well I know that God is nearer to me than to other artists; I associate with Him without fear; I have always recognized and understood Him and have no fear for my music—it can meet no evil fate. Those who understand it must be freed by it from all the miseries which the others drag about with themselves.

Music, verily, is the mediator between intellectual and sensuous life.

Speak to Goethe about me. Tell him to hear my symphonies and he will say that I am right in saying that music is the one incorporeal entrance into the higher world of knowledge which comprehends mankind but which mankind cannot comprehend.[28]

If we look at the ways of growth as ways toward fuller contact with reality, we at once see that all the important ones are paths to *experiencing,* without which reality can only be a concept or a fantasy. Psychoanalysts are aware that intellectual insight cannot substitute emotional insight. Gestalt therapists, even more aware of the screening effect of conceptual thinking, employ, instead of free association of thoughts, the exercise of staying in the continuum of awareness, much like that of sustained attention in meditative disciplines. In both meditation and Gestalt therapy there is a suppression of thinking and imagining in favor of sensing and feeling. Most meditative approaches stress the suppression of movement, so that attention and psychological activity are further channeled into the domain of pure receptivity. If objects are employed, attention is focused, not dispersed, so that it may reach beyond the ordinary schematic understanding. But sensory stimulation may also be withheld, which directs the person's consciousness more specifically to his inner events. We now know that extreme sensory deprivation can uncover the background of the person's feeling and his oneiric experience. The potential of this procedure has hardly been explored in the context of psychotherapy, but it seems like a hardy alternative to the longer though less drastic periods of sensory deprivation undergone by the early church fathers in the desert, by the Tibetan yogis in the Himalayas, or by the Eskimo shamans amid the polar ice.

We may discern different ingredients in the strategies that aim at the enhancement of experience, each of which is found in more than one of the more structured systems. One of these strategies can be seen as the *suppression of the filtering mechanisms* of our conscious mind. As Huxley pointed out, our perceptions are often more like gray illustrations of concepts than colors and shapes of the world—to say nothing of its smells and textures. We seem to take in as much of the world as we need to diagnose what is out there, which is all that our coping-oriented ego needs. Our total personality thirsts for more, though, and is left unsatisfied. To our greater self, sense impressions are the real food, not their conceptual labels. In his *The Psycho-Analysis of Artistic Vision and Hearing*, Anton Ehrenzweig posits that art gives us much food and manages to do so by means of a strategy that defeats our censorship: it keeps our conceptual mind busy with its own structure and regularity, while it speaks to our direct experiencing from its irregularity; by distracting our ego with its form, it reaches our unconscious from its formlessness.[29]

Another technique that may be regarded as an attempt to

bypass our ordinary conceptual filtering (aside from deliberate suppression of thinking as part of some practices) is the use of the tachistoscope that Professor Hoyt Sherman successfully employed as an artist-training tool.[30] If only given a fraction of a second to see the model, a painter will not be able to engage in the skilled but mechanical task of copying it, but will have to see the totality at once, and understand it instead of thinking about it. Studies quoted by Professor Samuel Renshaw claim that children improved at school and seemed to become more attentive when exposed to the task of seeing and drawing patterns projected with a tachistoscope.[31] I do not know of other studies along these lines, but it is conceivable that this approach may provide valuable training in openness toward the visual world and perhaps in sensory reality in general.

The psychedelic experience, too, can be seen as a device for the artificial suspension of filtering mechanism, as Huxley pointed out in *The Doors of Perception:*

> Reflecting on my experience, I find myself agreeing with the eminent Cambridge philosopher, Dr. C. D. Broad, "that we should do well to consider much more seriously than we have hitherto been inclined to do the type of theory which Bergson put forward in connection with memory and sense perception. The suggestion is that the function of the brain and nervous system and sense organs is in the main eliminative and not productive. Each person is at each moment capable of remembering all that has ever happened to him and of perceiving everything that is happening everywhere in the universe. The function of the brain and nervous system is to protect us from being overwhelmed and confused by this mass of largely useless and irrelevant knowledge, by shutting out most of what we should otherwise perceive or remember at any given moment, leaving only that very small and special selection which is likely to be practically useful." According to such theory, each one of us is potentially Mind at Large. But insofar as we are animals,

our business is at all costs to survive. To make biological survival possible, Mind at Large has to be funneled through the reducing valve of the brain and nervous system. What comes out at the other end is a measly trickle of the kind of consciousness which will help us to stay alive on the surface of this particular planet. To formulate and express the contents of this reduced awareness, man has invented and endlessly elaborated those symbol-systems and implicit philosophies which we call languages. Every individual is at once the beneficiary and the victim of the linguistic tradition into which he has been born—the beneficiary inasmuch as language gives access to the accumulated records of other people's experience, the victim insofar as it confirms him in the belief that reduced awareness is the only awareness and as it bedevils his sense of reality, so that he is all too apt to take his concepts for data, his words for actual things. That which, in the language of religion, is called "this world" is the universe of reduced awareness, expressed and, as it were, petrified by language. The various "other worlds" with which human beings erratically make contact are so many elements in the totality of the awareness belonging to Mind at Large. Most people, most of the time, know only what comes through the reducing valve and is consecrated as genuinely real by the local language. Certain persons, however, seem to be born with a kind of bypass that circumvents the reducing valve. In others, temporary bypasses may be acquired either spontaneously, or as the result of deliberate "spiritual exercises," or through hypnosis, or by means of drugs. Through these permanent or temporary bypasses there flows, not indeed the perception "of everything that is happening everywhere in the universe" (for the bypass does not abolish the reducing valve which still excludes the total content of Mind at Large), but something more than, and above all something different from, the carefully selected utilitarian material which our narrow individual minds regard as a complete, or at least sufficient, picture of reality.[32]

The concern with the surrender of the ego in mysticism may

be seen from the point of view under discussion as a stepping out of the way of a more direct apprehension of reality than the one which calls for conceptualization and the fitting of experiences into pre-established categories:

> To be a Sufi is to detach from fixed ideas and from preconceptions; and not to try to avoid what is your lot.
>
> —ABU-SAID, son of Abi Khain

> . . . I counsel that in the earnest exercise of mystical contemplation thou leave the senses and the operations of the intellect . . . and that thine understanding being laid to rest, thou ascend . . . towards union with Him whom neither being nor understanding can contain.
>
> —SAINT AUGUSTINE

An alternative way of contacting experience, used mostly in psychotherapy, is that of simply *pointing out* to the person his own processes. The forms of this reflexive and concentrative approach may vary. In analytical interpretations the reality that is pointed out may be unverifiable (experience must do that), so that the analyst arrives at it by intuition: "I think that you are regretting what you said," "I think that you are afraid," etc., but there is no clear demarcation between intuition or inference and the obvious facts. The Rogerian approach is more that of not going beyond the obvious, and merely *reflecting*. Such reflecting, experience shows, is not redundant but, just like the reflection from a mirror, adds another dimension to the person's experience of himself. In Gestalt therapy emphasis is placed on the patient's automatic or involuntary behavior, not for the purpose of interpretation but for *staying in touch* with the totality of the experience and *coming to the senses*.

A related strategy for contacting experience is that of *focusing*, which may be conceived as a self-reflecting, a pointing out of one's self, made possible by an exceptional effort of attention. Our experience occurs unconsciously to the extent that we are not directing our attention to it. It must be brought into focus, either by intentional vigilance (as in attending to feelings throughout a day, or in meditation periods), by the elimination of distractions, or by having it directed by another (as in reflecting).

A third way of bringing experience into focus is by identifying with or enacting certain emotions. The process of identifying with an object or character is implicit in the understanding of art (Theodor Lipp's and Worringer's "empathy," Polanyi's "indwelling"). In certain forms of meditation such identification is the deliberate goal. This may be looked at from the more obvious point of view of bringing about a temporary end to the subject-object dichotomy of discursive thinking (as distinct from intuitive thinking). But this is also a quality of experiencing as distinct from thinking. Not only are the aesthetic emotions a gratuitous enjoyment of the object in-itself and for-itself, but also in love and in the feeling of sacredness do we project ourselves into the being of the other and contact our own reality in the process. A form of meditation specifically linked to the activity of the artist is described in the following quotation:

> The artist (*sādhaka, mantrin,* or *yogin,* as he is variously and significantly called), after ceremonial purification, is to proceed to a solitary place. There he is to perform the "Sevenfold Office," beginning with the invocation of the hosts of Buddhas and Bodhisattvas, and the offering to them of real or imaginary flowers. Then he must realize in thought the four (infinite) modes of friendliness, compassion, sympathy, and impartiality. Then he must meditate upon the emptiness (*sunyata*) or non-existence of all things, for, "by the fire of the idea of the abyss, it is said, there are destroyed beyond recovery five factors" or ego-consciousness.

Then only should he invoke the desired divinity by the utterance of the appropriate seed-word (*bija*) and should identify himself completely with the divinity to be represented. Then finally, on pronouncing the *dhyāna mantra,* in which the attributes are defined, the divinity appears visibly, "like a reflection" or "as in a dream," and this brilliant image is the artist's model.[33]

It may be well to keep in mind a distinction between two meanings we ordinarily attribute to the word *identification.* In speaking of identification with a social role, for instance, we usually mean the substitution of our own experience with one compatible with such a role, much like the actor who forgets his everyday self while he identifies with his dramatic persona. In this way, too, children or grownups identify with parents, teachers, con men. But in contrast to this identification that is a substitution for another, there is one where the other (person, symbol, object, thought) acts like a vehicle for the expression and unfolding of the self. This takes place spontaneously in the course of life and is difficult to separate from the other form of identification. Significant persons (parents, teachers, admired ones) may become *models* in a way that is not compulsive and limiting but merely organizing, so that the individual assimilates stylistic elements of others as means for his own expression. This is the same process by which the great artist blends into his style the elements of his tradition, without being limited to them. This process may be understood as that of experiencing one's self in the guise of other—what is appreciated in the other and imitated was seen from the beginning as a tendency of one's self, i.e., what is assimilated is one's own projection.

In order to treat identification as a device for personal growth, one must choose objects that reflect the person's experience of himself, and thus constitute a symbol of him or of an aspect of him. One of the etymologies of *symbol* is *symballein*, "to throw together"; in this context, a symbol is a receptacle into which one can throw all his experiences. Such symbols are those of the one God in his different forms (in the Kabbalistic meditations on the names of God), of more particularized gods (in Tantric meditations) or "forces" (in much of esotericism), of the ideal man (the "imitation of Christ"), or of particular men.

Another starting point for the process of identification and experiencing may be a production of one's own, instead of an integrative symbol provided by tradition or fate. This is the case in the identification with archetypal contents in dreams or guided daydreams, the enactment of dreams in psychodrama, and the enactment of one's involuntary behavior in Gestalt therapy. In the latter instance the subject's task is to empathize with an action embodying an experience that he unconsciously must know, since it gave birth to the behavior. In *becoming* his body, he becomes what he already is. And what his *body* felt, *he* now feels.

The three approaches outlined above need not be regarded as incompatible, though each is stylistically clearcut when in quasi-pure form. Bypassing the filtering grid of ego, for instance, is a salient trait of meditative disciplines in general, for they all involve the development of receptivity. The reflexive and concentrative approach is prominent in the contemporary techniques of awareness, from the interpersonal to the physical ones (sensory awareness and movement therapy). The use of enactment as a means of access to a reality beyond the boundaries of ego is, by contrast, most characteristic of ritual forms.

All three may be found in a single tradition. Zen for instance has, along with its stress upon thoughtlessness and emptiness, a form of meditation that entails an enactment of the posture and attitude of the Buddha at the time of his enlightenment and uses concentration upon the breath and the experience of the moment. In encounter groups the aspect of suppression-of-suppression is seen, for example, in the requirement of avoiding intellectual allegations on judgments and opinions; reflecting takes place continuously through the verbalizations of the group leader or participants; and dramatic elements, some of which have been borrowed from Gestalt therapy and psychodrama, are used as specific techniques.

Deepening our contact with reality entails far more than a shift from conceptualization to experience. Once the veil of reason and pseudoreality is removed, there is still the path from illusion to reality, from assumptions and distorted images of reality (now exposed) to true contact. Behind the screens of the ego there are deeper screens, based on less conscious but greater fears. As a Zen story puts it, at the beginning of the journey the trees look like trees, the mountain looks like a mountain and the lake looks like a lake. In the middle of the journey the trees do not look like trees any more, the mountain does not look like a mountain, and the lake is no longer a lake. But at the end of the journey the trees look like trees, the mountain looks like a mountain, and the lake looks like a lake. At the beginning of the journey there is the pseudosanity of a merely intellectual knowledge that mountains are mountains, and the price of the rational view upon all personality is that of functional mutilation. In the middle of the journey there is acknowledged delusion and confusion. At this stage we can distinguish two avenues to the transformation of delusion into reality, compatible with each other and both present as components in a given approach.

One avenue is that of letting the delusional system "wear itself out" spontaneously as it is exposed to conscious scrutiny. Just as we may seize a dropping object as soon as we realize that it is falling, we naturally correct our views as soon as we make them clear enough to ourselves, generally in the process of expressing them to somebody else. This goes beyond verbal or conceptual notions, and is inseparable from a healthy life: we outgrow ourselves through reflective awareness and choice. The notion that self-expression itself can be constructive even when it only expresses the soul's "garbage," would be supported by most, but I think that it finds particularly clear expression in the following approaches: (1) Laing's "blow-out" approach to schizophrenia, where the process is respected as the person's deepest need and therapeutic move, and left to its natural course;[34] (2) the guided daydream, a process in the evolution of which childish and unrealistic fantasies move naturally in the direction of archetypal contents and a concern with the central issues of existence; [35] (3) Subud's *latihan** in which it is expected that expression "from within" will be self-perfecting, and nothing else is required but giving in to the preference of every moment. In all these and many more, the individual's experience is displayed for him to take it or leave it in an act of evaluation, so that whatever is invalid in it melts in the fire of consciousness.

The other avenue into reality, instead of attending to and expressing the area of delusion (symptoms, feelings, fantasies, or the stream of consciousness with its diverse ingredients), moves into reality and *squeezes it,* as it were, for more and more. This is the way of understanding, when rightly understood (as distinct from conceptual learning). Every drop of true understanding—which is experiential knowledge—kills some ghost in our fantasy life and opens up a way into the real, where we

* See p. 67.

may find further understanding. This is the way of the humanities, when put to their real purpose of showing man to man, the way of religious symbolism, and the way of art. A symbol, artistic or religious, is intended to re-create in the perceiver the experience that gave it birth but, paradoxically, it cannot be understood by other than he who has had the experience already. What the symbol does, then, is to bring certain experiences into focus—experiences that are at the core of our being human, and are inseparable from our reality. A symbol only arouses what is close to the surface of our consciousness, so we must find what is meaningful to us in our individual condition at the moment. As we move toward greater understanding and deeper experience, our appreciation of the symbolic world changes, and we need different books, different music, different forms to take us to the next step.

Among the symbolic means of conveying the attributes of reality, ritual holds a prominent place. All art is ritual in the sense that to experience it we must identify with it. But ritual is the deliberate acting out of symbolic forms, which stresses the process of identification. Naturally, it is possible to undergo a ritual in a mechanical way without the inner identification or empathy; this occurs so frequently that *ritualistic* has come to mean lifeless, without emotion or inner participation. Yet the essence of ritual is in the combination of an integrative symbol (an "archetype," Jung would say) and the technique of identification by means of which, in giving it our life, we may discover what our life is like.

Participation vs. Detachment

Be in the world, not of the world.
—Sufi saying

I am lumping together here under the heading of participation vs. detachment what might appear to be quite distinct issues—body vs. mind, selfhood vs. selflessness, doing vs. nondoing—because I think that they are only different aspects of the same thing and harder to separate from one another than from the other six aspects under which we are considering the single experience of change (that is, the *inner* action of the methods).*

Differences between these issues are greatest when we treat them as concepts. Instead, in terms of experience, being one's body, being the doer of one's actions, and perceiving one's self as substantially existing, constitute aspects of a single state, opposed to having a body, witnessing natural processes rather than doing them, seeing oneself as empty of any substantial being.

Neither of the states outlined above is that of average humanity, and in fact their description may generally appear as theoretical speculation rather than anything that can be experienced; we usually do not experience ourselves as *being* our body, but *living in* it, or *having* one. Our "true being"—regardless of our possible materialistic outlook in theory—feels more like that of a mind, consciousness, or soul *in* the body. Nor do we experience ourselves as doers of all our actions. Many things "happen" to us, and we are not our ultimate masters; we may do what we want, but we cannot *want* what we want. The very word *passion*—denoting the root of our actions—implies passivity; our impulses lead us, we do not feel that they stem from us. It is truer that we see ourselves as wanting; but not as wanting all our wants. In much of our lives we are aware of having wants that we do not want; our self and our urges are disassociated, just as self and body are. Who is it in

* See pp. 126–27.

us that says "I" and is not the body, or the passions, or what we do? Whoever pursues this meditation discovers that this "I" lacks substantial existence.

But we do not experience ourselves at the other end of the range either. If we fully experienced ourselves as not-the-body we would see our existence as independent of our body and feel invulnerable to any physical threat, particularly death. If we experienced everything as happening to us or happening through us, instead of it being our doing and choice, we would be able to surrender to the unavoidable stream of happening and cease our frantic striving to alter its course. If we felt completely detached from the stream of events in us and around us, too, we would hold no preference for this or that, and we would allow it to be as it is. As to the experience of being nonexistent, this may be hard even to imagine or conceive, so remote does it seem from our ordinary state of consciousness. When we look at the recipes for better living, though, mystical or secular, old or new, we cannot dispense with these issues. While implicit in some of the ways, they are very explicit in others.

Interestingly, too, we can see both extremes equally represented among the ways of growth: that of cultivating a sense of identity or oneness with the body, and that of developing the perception of self as a mind, spirit, or consciousness transcending the physical, for which the body is a mere outer garment or shell; that of promoting the realization that all our actions, even the automatic ones, are our doing and responsibility, and that of stressing that everything happens to us or through us and that we are unable to do anything; that of saying that we are one with everything, and that of saying that there is no such thing as an "I"; that of stressing that we are one with our impulses, and that of stressing that our true self or essence is above ephemeral wants, filled by itself.

All these antinomic positions could be summarized in two approaches: that which stresses the fullest participation in the processes of the organism and world (body, feelings, desires, and their consequences), and that which stresses detachment or disidentification from such processes. Furthermore, as I hope to show, these two approaches are only apparent opposites, and each may be realized only if it ceases to be understood as contradictory with the other. If not, we degenerate into blind asceticism and blind hedonism.

The I-am-the-body approach is implicit in the work of those who have contributed in recent years to the rediscovery of the physical aspects of psychotherapy and self-realization. Those who have studied with Charlotte Selver* will have heard from her lips, as I have, that "our body is important because we *are* our body", and we can all read similar statements in Stanley Keleman, a leading exponent of bioenergetic analysis. Interest in the body, though, is not merely a contemporary trend, nor a purely Western one. One of its most significant expressions, for instance, may be seen in the rise of *tantris* in India and Tibet.

The most consistent formulation and use of the "I-am-in-the-body" assumption in the current approaches is to be found in Gestalt therapy, and its examination in that context can show us more of its implications. For the Gestalt therapist, all that happens in us *we do,* but we do not acknowledge or experience this as such, for we dis-identify ourselves from our processes; we create a fictitious barrier between "I" and "it," call-

* Charlotte Selver introduced the label "sensory awareness" for the discipline originated in the work of her teacher, Elsa Gindler. Elsa Gindler simply called her activity *Arbeit am Menschen* (work on people) and, to my knowledge, never committed the system to writing. In spite of the extent of present interest in this discipline and the growing number of people involved in its teaching, the available bibliography does not go beyond two articles.[36]

ing non-ego everything for which we do not want to take responsibility. The goal of therapy, from one point of view, is that of making us realize that we are where we want to be, that we are doing what we want to do, that we are going in the direction of our preference—which we enjoy! All this, however, we do not normally acknowledge, not in full measure at least. We stand outside ourselves, identifying with a fictitious I to whom all *happens*.

The practical consequences of this point of view bear on each domain of psychological functioning. First, the patient is urged to change his way of speaking about himself in the direction of *I-language*. This entails the practice of saying "I think" rather than "the thought occurs to me," "I itch in my arm" rather than "my arm itches," "I let my mind wander" rather than "my mind wanders." Likewise, the word *it* is avoided whenever possible and substituted by *I* or *you*, and also avoided is the use of *one* or *you* to denote impersonality (*you* would not think so, etc.). The mere shift in language entails a shift in point of view and, like a ritual, brings along an experiential *as if*: it invites the person to experience himself as if he were the responsible doer of his actions and the locus of his perceptions, so that he may have a chance of discovering that this is indeed "true" (i.e., an experiential fact).

The same "as if" approach is made to bear directly on the issue of being one's body in the practice of *becoming* the body, its parts or actions, by giving it words or simply effecting an imaginary shift in identity. A patient may be instructed to "play" his voice, for instance, or his left hand, or his smile, and this may eventually lead him to discover his own feelings and "doing" in all that before had seemed to him automatic, meaningless, and feelingless. What the body felt, knew, and wanted, *he* now feels, knows, and wants. The ego has extended his frontiers, but only in the person's reowning the disavowed and realizing that such frontiers were a myth to begin with.

What are the limits of this approach? If I am my body, feelings, thoughts, wishes; if I am (and I do) whatever I may call my processes, where are my limits? For my processes are certainly not limited by my skin. The events within me are fragments in causal chains that originate beyond me and do not end in me. All there is is a universal stream of causality, and only arbitrarily or for practical purposes do I call *me* the region of my body.

Yet, though "I" digest my food and renew my skin, I, personally, am not aware of doing so. Though awareness may expand and a person may extend the boundaries of his "I" to include more of himself and more of the world, there is a habitual boundary that few claim to trespass. Again, this is the boundary between the therapeutic endeavor and the mystical. The psychotherapist speaks of becoming conscious, but would not think of (or be interested in) becoming conscious of the vegetative or cellular processes. The mystic claims to grow his "I-amness" to the size of the world.

"Tat tvam asi," say the Upanishads: "Thou art That." Everything in the world is of the same substance as you—more, it *is* you. "Wherever you turn your face, there is God," says the Koran, referring again to the oneness of everything. The individual is only a facet of that oneness—or else a nothingness, an illusion.

Let us now examine the alternative approach, that of disidentification from the body and phenomena. It may be found in modern systems, such as psychosynthesis,[37] but it is at least as old as Patanjali's yoga. For Patanjali[38] the self is *enmeshed* in the psychic structure, but is different from it. "I" am not only not my body, but I am not my feelings nor my thoughts. All these occur in me, and I mistakenly identify myself with them. Believing I am them, I become attached to them and fear harm or loss. But nothing could really harm "me" or even touch me or affect me, for I am beyond the mechanicalness of physical and mental processes. The Hindu formula for the discovery of the self is *neti neti,* "not that, not that." For "self" cannot possibly be described in positive terms, though it is the heart of everything. Whatever may be pointed at, it is not. The relevant psychological exercise stemming from this approach is the perfect opposite of the identification or enactment procedure in Gestalt therapy. It is one of sensing the body in the attitude of "this is my body, not me"; contemplating the emotions and feelings in that of "these feelings occur in me, but are not myself, I can exist without them"; and regarding thoughts in the same way: "here is a thought that I have; it is not me."

Naturally, the practice of this approach leads to less vulnerability, greater inner freedom, less attachment to particular feeling states or opinions and therefore greater flexibility, all in the direction of mental health.

If we carry the thought (and, we are told, the experience) to its ultimate consequences, though, we will see the domain of the self shrinking more and more as we deprive it of all we regarded as part of it—until it vanishes into nothing. And again we find ourselves in the domain of mystical experience and its formulations.

The experience of self as ultimately nothing has been expressed most explicitly in Buddhism, which holds this realization as the heart of enlightenment. Nirvana is extinction not only of desire but of self. The doctrine of no-self (*Anatta*), which probably found its most systematic exponent in the Indian philosopher Nagarjuna (about 113–213 A.D.), is a very salient feature of the Mahayana school of Buddhism. The central voidness of our nature is depicted in Tibet as a diamond, for it is at once most transparent, bright, hard, and enduring. The Chinese Zen patriarch Hui-neng, emphasizing the quality of emptiness, compares mind to space:

> The capacity of the mind is as great as that of space. It is infinite, neither round nor square, neither great nor small, neither green nor yellow, neither red nor white, neither above nor below, neither long nor short, neither angry nor happy, neither right nor wrong, neither good nor evil, neither first nor last. All Buddha Ksetras (lands) are as void as space. Intrinsically our transcendental nature is void and not a single Dharma can be attained. It is the same with the Essence of Mind, which is a state of "Absolute Void" (*i.e.* the voidness of non-void).[39]

The experience of self-as-nothingness filled by the world (or by God) is not confined to Buddhism. Christianity abounds with utterances from the mystics that express the same view, and in Islam we find that the term for "enlightenment" is practically a translation of Nirvana: *fanā-f'illah* extinction. The theme of emptiness pervades Lao Tzu's Tao Te Ching:

> Tao is empty like a bowl
> It may be used but its capacity is never exhausted.
>
> Infinite and boundless, it cannot be given any name:
> It returns to nothingness.

Or:

> A pot is made out of clay,
> But emptiness constitutes its essence.[40]

Consequently, the best rulers are "subtly mysterious," "genuine like a piece of uncarved wood," "open and broad," "like a valley," "merged and undifferentiated," "like muddy water."

As being-the-body implies being desires, being-no-thing implies standing aside from desires: they are part of the body, part of the universal stream of events, but they are not *me*. Therefore the injunction of the *Bhagavad Gītā* of being the same in pleasure and in pain. And as being-in-the-body entails being the doer of actions, the extinction of apparent existence amounts to a non-doing, a transparence, and a letting go to what is: God's will, *dharma,* Tao. Yet this state is not depicted as one of indifference but, on the contrary, a desireless and gratuitous bliss. It is a saying yes to the inevitability of happenings, a relinquishing of preferences, and an equal love for everything. The following story is illustrative of this attitude:

> The Zen master Hakuin was praised by his neighbours as one living a pure life.
>
> A beautiful Japanese girl whose parents owned a food store lived near him. Suddenly, without any warning, her parents discovered she was with child.
>
> This made her parents angry. She would not confess who the man was, but after much harassment at last named Hakuin.
>
> In great anger the parents went to the master. "Is that so?" was all he would say.
>
> After the child was born it was brought to Hakuin. By this time he had lost his reputation, which did not trouble him, but he took very good care of the child. He obtained milk from his neighbours and everything else the little one needed.
>
> A year later the girl-mother could stand it no longer. She told her parents the truth—that the real father of the child was a young man who worked in the fishmarket.
>
> The mother and father of the girl at once went to Hakuin to ask his forgiveness, to apologize at length, and to get the child back again.
>
> Hakuin was willing. In yielding the child, all he said was: "Is that so?" [41]

Though logically opposite, the ideas of self as everything or nothing may be only alternative translations of a single experience into the medium of concepts and words. Many formulations, indeed, insist that the reality which is talked about transcends both predicaments. *The Tibetan Book of the Dead* reads: "Recognizing the voidness of thine own intellect to be Buddhahood, and knowing it at the same time to be thine own consciousness, thou shalt abide in the state of the divine mind of the Buddha."

Also, whether the I is experienced as the all or as nothing, one consequence is the same: the distinction between "self" and "other" disappears. In both cases, all that *exists* is one.

I have already quoted James Jeans's reflection upon the irreconcilable models of light as wave or as particles, both of which explain certain phenomena, and his suggestion that this may be the consequence of trying to represent in our minds a reality of more dimensions than we can grasp.* In many of our conceptual models we pay a price for translating something into a lower dimensional medium, and for translating its ineffability into the logical medium through which we communicate. So, in order to speak of the experience of the most desirable state that is the object of the most ambitious quests, we may have to accept its rendering through paradoxes. The paradox is the ultimate that reason can apprehend. Standing with one foot on each side of the paradox, one may be able to get his head beyond it. I am therefore suggesting that along with the conceptual duality of being all and nothing we can conceive an experiential monism in terms of which the antithetical conceptions are equally true. Mahayana Buddhism states it: nirvana equals samsara!

We do not have to meet a living Buddha to find the rele-

* See p. 91.

vance of these antithetical experiences to life. For, as a Buddhist would say, each one of us is the living Buddha, and the experience of enlightenment is the one we are having right now, only we have not found it out. In all experience we can see our doing or non-doing, our selfhood or selflessness, our responsible choice or total irresponsibility, and to the extent that we find the one we find the other. This is more evident the greater the experience itself, so we can see it best in peak-experiences. Take love as an example. We can describe it as one when we forget ourselves and melt with the loved one or the world. And yet it is at the same time a state of enchanted I-ness, selfhood. Or take the experience of orgasm. It has been described in terms of dissolution or death, and yet it may also be seen as a peak of aliveness and presence. Such is the quality of awareness in general—the more noteworthy, the greater the awareness. It is a state of contact with a not-I, even an immersion in a not-I, which, in the heightened awareness of aesthetic or religious perception, becomes alive with I-qualities. And, being a self-forgetfulness in the contemplation of the object, a state of being-through-the-object, or being-in-the-sensation, it is also a state of self-remembrance and enhanced presence. The simultaneity of these opposites as a way of life may be recognized in the advice of a Japanese Zen Master to the effect of living "with an empty heart" so that it may be filled by the world, or in the Sufi dictum of being "*in* the world but not *of* the world."

I have pointed out the connection between the approach of Gestalt therapy and the view of the person as totally responsible for and identical with his processes. Whenever he reaches the goal, however—not the definitive one but the limited goal of a shift in the perception of a given behavior, and a patient, for instance, discovers how he is worrying through being worried, or wants to move away from somebody rather than feeling overcome by irrational discomfort and boredom—then the paradoxical happens: he can stop if he chooses. Just as knowledge of the external world gives him power, self-knowledge, in the form of direct experience of his processes, gives him control. And so he identifies with his being, enters into his processes, and at the same time rises above himself, feels free from his processes, detached as the master is from the horse.

What seems to be a way of *descent* into the body and the senses ends up by being a way of *ascent* to the spiritual domain of consciousness and freedom. I think that the same may be said of all the ways of descent. Perhaps the most impressive means of bringing out man-the-animal is effected through the administration of ibogaine, and results in finding, at the core of "animal" urges, a "wanting more" which in its undifferentiated form is identical with "religious" longing. Paradoxically, deepening sensuous or instinct-bound experience by *entering* it transforms its perception so that it loses much of what we ordinarily call sensuous. Thus the practice of sensory awareness, by the simple focusing of attention on physical processes, frequently leads to peak-experiences or psychedelic-like states, just as in meditation. In tantra yoga the strategy of descending in order to ascend is most explicit. Its philosophy is that what binds us may free us—the body, the instincts, and particularly the sexual drive. All these approaches lead to what has been symbolically depicted as the descent into our underworld, that Orpheus (the artist), Eneas (the hero), or Saint Paul (the mystic) must undertake—a process that Dante described in the first person on his way to Beatrice and the heavenly spheres. We can look at it either as *tat tvam asi*—"this is myself"—or alternatively and simultaneously as *neti neti*—"this is not me: you are there, I am here, you are only *in* me, not my essential nature."

We can say the same of psychoanalysis. It is really a descent into the mind's underworld, and as it unfolds before the patient's conscious gaze he experiences at the same time two facets of awareness: "here is another part of me," and "here is something that was driving me from behind, and now I can see its face; I can set myself above it."

By the same token, we can look at the ways of ascent as an effort to detach from the body the feelings, the mental processes; as implicit ways of descent into contact with such processes. For detachment is only possible in such contact, in the moment when we can say: "Aha! Here is *this*—and it is not me." Since there is no *I* without *that*, the process of finding one's self becomes one of self-observation. We can find it most clearly in the Buddhist cultivation of mindfulness. In fact, the contemplation of the body that is part of such practice appears to be identical in spirit to that of contemporary sensory awareness, though the former is formulated in the context of disidentification and the latter in that of identification with the body. Consider for instance, the following paragraph by a Ceylonese monk, Nyaponika Thera:

> In the general application of this exercise, during one's routine life, its first purpose is to increase the awareness of one's momentary bodily behaviour when going, standing, sitting or reclining. It frequently happens that the preoccupation with thoughts about the *aim* of going, completely blots out the full consciousness of the *act* of going; and that, through giving sole attention to the activity performed while standing or sitting, there may be no conscious awareness of those two postures themselves. Though, in ordinary life, it will neither be possible nor even desirable to be always fully conscious of the postures, neverthleless a practice of this awareness of postures will be wholesome for many practical reasons too. By directing one's attention to the posture, any nervous haste in going will be restrained; unnecessary and harmful distortions of the body, in the case of the other postures, will be avoided, or cor-

rected, and thereby those postural defects with which medical science has to deal in the case of children, and adults too, will be prevented. Unnecessary fatigue of the body, and, consequently, of mind, will be avoided, and reduction of the range of conscious control over the body prevented. Controlled movement of the body is necessarily an expression of a self-possessed mind.[42]

We can find another expression of the *neti neti* approach in the practice of schools established by Gurdjieff's students.* As in Buddhism and in most of psychotherapy, the emphasis is on watchfulness over physical, emotional, and mental processes and, particularly, sustained watchfulness throughout the day. An "observer" must develop, who can say to every complex or sub-self, "there you are: you are not I, you are just a part claiming to be the whole." In practice, the seeker finds out that he cannot be present always as an observer; there are gaps in his awareness. And as he tries further, he may discover that he has been avoiding the acknowledgment of aspects of his being that are expressed by certain actions, fantasies, or thoughts. Being present as an observer implies contacting these events, realizing not only that they are not him but that they are part of him *in* him.

Like other approaches stressing detached observation, the Gurdjieffian bears the mark of an ascetic tendency—opposition to the spontaneous processes may be an occasion for knowing them better.

Fusion, inner unity, is obtained by means of "friction," by the struggle between "yes" and "no" in man. If a man lives without inner struggle, if everything happens in him without opposition, if he goes wherever he is drawn or wherever the wind blows, he will remain such as he is. But if a struggle begins in him, and particu-

* The practical side of this system is not explicitly described in any book, but the interested reader may find the main ideas put forward in P. D. Ouspenski's *In Search of the Miraculous*[43] and De Ropp's *The Master Game*.[44]

larly if there is a definite line in this struggle, then, gradually, permanent traits begin to form themselves, he begins to "crystallize." [45]

This suggests that the process of asceticism, which may seem to be one of moving away from sensory experience, when rightly understood is one of facilitating real contact with the body and its artificially changed needs. The most effective way of rising above the senses and emotions is inseparable from the descent into direct contact with the immediacy of feeling.

Freedom vs. Necessity

> By definition, nibbana is therefore freedom from the
> emotions and desires by which egoism and attachment is
> created: all definitions are in complete agreement on this
> point. This does not mean complete absence of motivation,
> nor passivity.[46]

As in the previous section, I am discussing here some issues that are only apparently distinct: freedom vs. necessity, control vs. expression, and desire vs. needlessness. Not only are these issues intimately related among themselves, but, as we shall see, they are hard to treat without reference to those discussed in the previous sections—for the question of freedom is only another way of formulating the question of "who" (if anybody) is the doer of actions, and the issue of freedom is inseparable from that of identity.

Freedom is a goal of psychotherapy in more than one way. At the most obvious level, psychotherapy seeks a freedom from suffering. Beyond this, psychotherapy aims at freeing from disease—psychoneurosis, generally, that is conceived to be somewhat like an alter ego—a system of motivations, a false identity, a complex Gestalt of perceptual and behavioral modes, an enemy that man carries in himself, not unlike the devil of myth. In a still different but compatible sense, the successful psychotherapeutic process involves (both in the long run and in each micro-breakthrough) the attainment of an experience of freedom in which the individual perceives himself as unobstructed by himself and as an active force in the shaping of his life. This is the opposite of the loss of freedom that accompanies psychopathological conditions and that is particularly evident in the clearcut extreme of psychosis. In common parlance (and in the law) a sick person is not held "responsible."

The process of liberation entailed by psychotherapy has been conceptualized in different ways. In the orthodox Freudian view, emphasis lies in the overcoming of the past; freedom is freedom from patterns of reaction that were established in childhood and are no longer adequate to the present demands of reality. Going one step further along the Freudian path, Horney stresses that all neurotic needs are compulsive in that they constitute an escape from or solution to anxiety. The roots of anxiety, in turn, are seen in the unrealistic perception of self and environment and in the conflicts established in early life.

From another point of view, many have stressed the neurotic's lack of freedom resulting from his exaggerated dependency upon others, his inability to stand on his own or "do his own thing," his investing external sources of authority with sacrosanct powers while relinquishing his own sense of responsibility. The situation becomes even worse when this transfer of authority or direction involves the swallowing whole of the contradictions of our culture. As Barry Stevens puts it:

> In the beginning was I, and I was good.
> Then came in other I. Outside authority. This was confusing. And then other I became *very* confused because there were so many different outside authorities.

Sit nicely. Leave the room to blow your nose. Don't do that, that's silly. Why, the poor child doesn't even know how to pick a bone! Flush the toilet at night because if you don't it makes it harder to clean. DON'T FLUSH THE TOILET AT NIGHT—you wake people up! Always be nice to people. Even if you don't like them, you mustn't hurt their feelings. Be frank and honest. If you don't tell people what you think of them, that's cowardly. Butter knives. It is important to use butter knives. Butter knives? What foolishness! Speak nicely. Sissy! Kipling is wonderful! Ugh! Kipling (turning away).

The most important thing is to have a career. The most important thing is to get married. The hell with everyone. Be nice to everyone. The most important thing is sex. . . . The most important thing is to have everyone like you.[47]

To deal with this kind of situation, psychotherapy may involve leading the individual, at least temporarily, to a condition not unlike that described in Christ's statement, "The father shall be divided against the son, and the son against the father; the mother against the daughter, and the daughter against the mother; the mother in law against her daughter in law, and the daughter in law against her mother in law."

When we move from the psychotherapeutic domain to that of the spiritual disciplines, the idea of freedom is even more explicit. In *Psychotherapy East and West* Watts speaks of Buddhism, Vedanta, and Taoism as "ways of liberation," as they achieve the "release of the individual from forms of conditioning imposed upon him by social institutions."[48] In choosing this expression as a generic term for the Asian traditions, Watts follows the traditional Hindu designation of what Hinduism regards as one of the four aims of life: *Mukti,* liberation, deliverance.*

* The classical "four aims" spoken of in Hinduism are wealth (*artha*), pleasure or love (*kāma*), virtue (*dharma*), and liberation (*mukti*).

In the Christian conception, too, free will is man's lot to the extent that he shares the Divine nature. The struggle for freedom from the fetters of illusion and ego-sense in their multifarious manifestations (pride, craving or attachment, anger) is what gives to the traditional ways much of their character of disciplines in the sense of their being inner struggles. The language or the symbolism in which this unseen warfare is expressed vary according to time and place: freedom from "sin," from "ignorance," from "temptation," etc. Through centuries of blind usage, most of these words have acquired such deteriorated meaning that we may have trouble in recapturing the original meaning in which they all meet. *Sin,* for instance, in the Greek of the gospels means "missing the mark"—an expression borrowed from archery to indicate man's deviation from his true function and purpose. Freedom from sin in that sense means a freedom from those forces that impinge on man's consciousness, compelling him to be other than himself. This meaning is similar to that of "psychological health" for those who define it as the absence of symptoms. In behavior therapy, especially, the aim of treatment is to liberate the individual from conditionings that conflict with the intelligent satisfaction of his needs or the demands of reality.

Psychology has been increasingly aware of there being not only a freedom-from but a *freedom-for.* Sanity is not only in the absence of absolute and automatic responses to life, but in the pursuit of positive goals and in the manifestation of positive interests that are the source of our real preferences and choices. As Erich Fromm has shown in *Escape from Freedom,*[49] this is a prerogative that men easily lose sight of and give up, substituting for it a slavery to external or internalized authority, or mass narcotizations. It is of this freedom-for that Rogers speaks when he refers to

. . . an experience on which I have placed various labels as I have tried to think about it—becoming a person, freedom to be, courage to be, learning to be free—yet the experience is something broader than, and deeper than, any of its labels.

. . . The experience to which I am referring is a central process or central aspect of psychotherapy. It is the experience of becoming a more autonomous, more spontaneous, more confident person. It is the experience of freedom to be one's self.

He quotes some statements from clients to convey what he means:

"I'm *not* the sweet forbearing guy that I try to make out that I am. I get irritated at things. I feel like snapping at people, and I feel like being selfish at times; and I don't know why I should pretend I'm *not* that way."

"I've always tried to be what the others thought I should be, but now I'm wondering whether I shouldn't just see that I am what I am."

"I don't know *what* I'm gonna do, but *I'm* gonna do it." [50]

The vision of a positive freedom—a freedom-for—is as explicit in the language of religion as in that of psychology. If we turn to it now and ask what is left to man once his obstacles are removed, the answer is that it is not chaos or random behavior, but quite the opposite: the person's essential stream of choices and preferences (his being true to himself) is most coherent and articulate, and bears the mark of his unique style. In this sense, our freedom is that of being what we are—a giving in to the *necessity* of our being. (In the writings of Saint Paul, freedom, equated with freedom from sin, is equivalent to living in Christ.) The Christian's freedom to live "in Christ" is equivalent to that of utmost obedience to "God's will," just as in Mohammedanism the free man is one who becomes a "slave of God." *

* Alan Watts comments upon this paradox of freedom in surrender in his introduction to Spiegelberg's *Spiritual Disciplines of India.*[51]

Leaving aside all speculation about determinism-indeterminism, we can safely say that the experiential characteristic of the higher states in the ladder of human inner attainment may be described as one of freedom or of surrender. God's Law, *dharma,* Tao,* the Way, all point to a precise course of action which is for man to follow whenever he is "free" for it. "The spirit is freedom," said Hegel, but he conceived freedom as the acceptance of necessity; and Buber said of the free man that he "believes in his destiny." Fully aware of this apparent paradox, Carl Rogers writes: "Freedom, rightly understood, is a fulfillment, by the person, of the ordered sequence of his life."

From what has been said in the preceding pages, it is clear that the issue of freedom is no other than that of being one's self. It is once more the issue of identity, but from a different perspective that takes into account the pressure of the forces of inauthenticity and the need of what Paul Tillich called a "courage to be." Also, being or living one's truth presupposes the knowing of one's truth: having that direct self-knowledge that we discussed as the issue of reality vs. illusion. To surrender is in the first place surrendering to one's experience rather than repressing it or distorting it: being open.

The quality of freedom also distinguishes voluntary acts from actions that are involuntary or automatic. Since voluntary actions are carried out consciously, this issue is inseparable from that of consciousness. In similar fashion the freedom to be one's self is inseparable from an attitude of self-acceptance. Both converge upon that way of life that Thomas Merton has described as the person's "freedom from concern that goes with being simply what he is and accepting things as they are in order to work with them as he can." [52]

---

* As dharma, Tao has various levels of significance. Every being has his Tao or Way, and beyond that there is the Tao of the world—Universal Law.

An issue which is related to freedom is that of ease—and its counterpart, difficulty, "work." Letting go of our essential nature, surrendering to the stream of our experience may be considered as the position of least effort; in fact such experience of being carried or being one with the flow of life events is often depicted in the East as one of *wu wei,* non-doing. Yet spontaneity involves the contradiction of the whole of our conditioned personality—a going against the grain of inner obstacles. And in that sense it is hard work. The word *yoga* derives from a root meaning "yoke," which is interesting for its double meaning— on one hand, it indicates the condition of becoming yoked to the self, attaining union. On the other, a yoke conveys the notion of burden and heavy work. What is the greatest ease from the point of view of the essence is also the greatest difficulty for the ego-centered personality. Literally, it means its sacrifice and surrender. And what may be seen as a simultaneous process of "letting go" and "working against" from the contrasting points of view of the self and the programed robot in us, may also be seen as a course of personal growth in which one process follows the other. What to the beginner is effort, "austerities," self-discipline, is pursued for its intrinsic reward by a more advanced person. Thus, truth can only be expressed at the beginning of psychotherapy by an effort to overcome feelings of shame and guilt, going against the stream of ordinary propensities—by resisting. Yet a healthy person feels that it is an effort to be roundabout, and that truth "makes him free." Real communication, which may be achieved only by resisting fear of rejection, becomes natural, and work in general takes on the nature of play.

Lack of freedom is equated with the experience of viewing one's self as the moved rather than the mover, that is, as removed, disassociated from one's own processes. Complete merging with one's processes, instead, involves identification with the mover—an experience of will. The stance or state of participation-in-detachment that we have described can also be seen as one of letting one's reality be—letting it be free and being free from it at the same time.

The angle of freedom may be used to look at the different means of self-transformation as ways of training in freedom or in surrender, and from this point of view such techniques may be classified under three types.

One is that comprising procedures of liberation from conditioning or automatisms and, in a certain sense, from desires in general. It is the *via purgativa* of mystical traditions, which coincides in general terms with what we have called the way of ascent and detachment. It is a negative way, one of elimination or overcoming, and its discussion overlaps that of asceticism.

In a second approach to inner freedom the emphasis lies in the positive surrender to one's being, structure, and destiny. This is the domain of attunement to one's deepest promptings, the cultivation of spontaneity and expression. Just as the negative way is one of pursuing a freedom from false identity, from infectious delusions and obstacles to one's true nature, the positive way is the complementary pursuit of that surrender to one's true nature (or to the life stream as embodied in one's self) which can in turn liberate us from compulsive social games or character formations.

The third type of technique is characterized by its structured quality. Like the negative way, this approach involves the assumption that for change to take place the present personality must be left behind. But since the alternative to man's present conditioning cannot be known to him in his conditioned state, he is provided with models that contain indications as to how to act, think, and feel, which may constitute a prefiguration of his still unexpressed authenticity. In carrying out actions or thinking thoughts that fall outside his habitual system of function, but that are mere responses to an external prescription, the person may have occasion, first, to make himself free for them (i.e., develop enough flexibility or noncompulsiveness in his personality) and, second, discover that these are closer to expressing *his own* tendencies or views. Understandably, only a guide of great human knowledge and intuition may be able to see and suggest the suppressed action that would make another person more complete and more himself —but this type of individual prescription is an important element of spiritual guidance in most cultures, as well as inspired good advice in ordinary human relations. However, even the authority vested upon a guide may be insufficient to counteract the ingrained tendencies that the person needs to overcome:

One day a man reproached Bayazid, the great mystic of the ninth century, saying that he had fasted and prayed and so on for thirty years and not found the joy which Bayazid described. Bayazid told him that he might continue for three hundred years and still not find it.

"How is that?" asked the would-be illuminate.

"Because your vanity is a barrier to you."

"Tell me the remedy."

"The remedy is one which you cannot take."

"Tell me, nevertheless."

Bayazid said: "You must go to the barber and have your (respectable) beard shaved. Remove all your clothes and put a girdle around yourself. Fill a nosebag with walnuts and suspend it from your neck. Go to the marketplace and call out: 'A walnut will I give to any boy who will strike me on the back of the neck.' Then continue on to the justices' session so that they may see you."

"But I cannot do that; please tell me something else that would do as well."

"This is the first move, and the only one," said Bayazid, "but I had already told you that you would not do it; so you cannot be cured." [53]

An alternative to the individual prescription is the structuring of life after universal models, that is, indications of how to act, think, and feel which allow for one's individuality to partake in the general qualities of life as lived by those who have attained their goal. Life is patterned after rules or precepts, sentiments are shaped with prayer or with the deliberate suppression of negative feelings, and with the cultivation of love; thinking is patterned after symbols expressive of universal truths. It is expected that all such crutches may sustain the new man until he can walk by himself, and he will eventually find that the images or rules (provided from without) anticipated the preferences and perceptions of his deeper being. This rationale is understandable, yet we should not be blind to its risk. In religions symbols have often replaced truth, norms tend to become the very life of the individual, and crutches in general substitute the legs to the point that they atrophy completely.

If we look panoramically at the ways from the point of view of this threefold classification, we note that the prescriptive approach is that of religious forms; the ascetic is more specifically a mystical path, and the expressive-cathartic (or spontaneous) is predominant in psychotherapy and art.*

The case of psychoanalysis is almost too obvious to need much elaboration. *Free* association is both the tool and the symbol of the person's condition. The analytical process is one of attaining greater ego-permissiveness: the freedom to feel one's own feelings, allow for one's urges, contact one's spontaneous functions. And aside from a matter of emphasis, which

* This distinction should not be exaggerated, though. The individual prescriptive approach is the essence of behavior therapy, for instance, and spontaneity is a major aspect of Subud.

may be on thinking and remembering, on imagining, or on feeling and sensing, there is not too great a difference between progress in free association, meditation, the practice of self-awareness, Gestalt therapy, or the guided daydream. They all constitute the challenge of letting go, surrendering to the stream of psychic events, achieving the necessary freedom from interference, censorship, or distractions to letting it happen.

In the same light we may consider the ways of spontaneity in movement, from the less structured ones like improvisational dance to the highly structured ones like the Japanese tea ceremony; or the ways of spontaneity in human contact such as encounter groups, psychodrama, and synanon games; or in the reception of impressions from our bodies and the environment as in sensory awareness; or in the handling of color, shapes, and symbolic forms in art education. Freedom is freedom to know and freedom to do. Its fruits are, on the cognitive side, the Delphic "know thyself" that can only be attained by relinquishing filtering mechanisms and daring to see; and on the active side, the Shakespearean "to thine own self be true" that entails the relinquishing of social automatisms and the courage to be.

If the danger in the way of self-denial is that of suppressing the healthy along with the unhealthy, the danger in spontaneity is represented by a delusion of freedom stemming from accord to deeply rooted conditionings, instead of the freedom from conditioning which is sought. In both cases, blind procedures cannot lead to the goal, and the intuition of the living guide cannot be dispensed with.

The ascetic and the prescriptive approaches are more compatible with one another than with the expressive, and I believe that the contrast between these and the latter lies behind much of the doubt felt about one another by partisans of the "spiritual" and of the "medical" approaches. The therapist cannot believe that anything coming from without may be other than a strait jacket, while the religious man is prone to project God's will into a transcendent order and to expect no more than chaos from the law of man's heart. In their unenlightened forms, religion is one-sidedly Apollonian and psychotherapy one-sidedly Dionysian. And taken at face value, the freedoms of which they speak may seem to be two opposite freedoms: from desires in one case, and from constraint in the other.

The notion of liberation as a moving away from desiring is only another aspect of that which we already touched upon as detachment, and once more we should seek to understand the experiential foundation of this idea if we want to avoid getting stuck in dogmatic assertions or denials. Moreover, it is most likely that the struggle against the passions, that is so intimately linked to the story of civilization, is not the outcome of either ideology or psychosocial dynamics but the experience of individuals who have come to a state of blissful cessation of cravings and found "renunciation of the world" to be their most natural state. The existence of such a state of apparent needlessness may be said to be an implicit assumption of asceticism. For instance, in giving up the pursuit of their physical pleasures, the fathers in the desert knew well the existence of "pleasures" of another order—the fullness of contemplation, in which the soul is filled by itself. Further removed from the experience, other ascetics imitated the fathers' actions, deeming them "virtuous" by themselves. In recent times Puritanism made a whole people believe in the evilness of instinct.

The experience of needlessness, though, continues to take place in the life of individuals regardless of their beliefs and expectations. Maslow, for instance, writing about peak-experiences remarked that in them the individual, "because he becomes more unmotivated, that is to say, closer to non-striving, non-needing, non-wishing, he asks less for himself." Also, he sees the world in an "ego-transcending self-forgetful, egoless, unselfish" way. "It can come closer to being unmotivated, impersonal, desireless, detached, not needing or wishing." His cognition is such that he tends to perceive external objects, the world, and individual people as more *detached from human concerns*. . . . The perceiver can more readily look upon nature as if it were there in itself and for itself, not merely as if it were a human playground put there for human purposes.

Aside from peak-experiences which, as self-validating and far-reaching in the life of the individual as they may be, are relatively rare, there is an experience which may be thought of as the intimation of its possibility—that in which the individual longs for something hitherto unexperienced and perhaps indefinite, but distinctly other than his "worldly" concerns. He has, so to speak, given up all his desires save one. When this longing is intense and the intimation of the possible is most clear, we are in the presence of true religiosity, in the sense meant, for instance, by André Festugière: "The religious man is he who senses, beyond earthly things, a Presence and who needs to feel that Presence. For, let him cease to feel it, and all is emptiness, the world is no more than a desert in which he is lost." [54]

But is this not, to some extent, the condition of most men? Is the human situation not like that of the sick princess in the fairy tale who languishes and ceases to eat since she has fallen in love with a distant prince? According to the story, her interest in the world is restored only after a wise man diagnoses the hidden source of her malady and the king brings the lovers together.

Maslow introduced a distinction between *deficiency motivations* like hunger or security and *growth motivations,* and remarked that the satiation of the former may be conducive to the expression of the latter. In the story of the princess, though, as in asceticism, we have an instance of a growth motivation that not only continues to exist in the face of a frustration of deficiency needs, but is the source of their voluntary frustration.

Just as we can see a relative needlessness in peak-experiences and in the spontaneous diminution in greed and ambition which may be associated with the redirecting of psychic energy toward the goal of self-actualization, we can also find it as an expression of psychological maturity and health.

Perls's contention that maturation is in the development of self-support instead of external support refers not only to a freedom from interpersonal dependencies, but to a psychological process not unlike the Buddhistic "extinction of desires." An ideal of desirelessness, just as asceticism, runs counter to the views of Western man, and Buddhism in particular (though not ascetic) has often been called life-denying. Is not desire at the root of all life? Yet the experience of desirelessness does not imply the cessation of life functions, but, rather, a joy in the given with no craving for what is not. The essence of such experience lies not in a cessation of impulses but in a different stance of the individual's consciousness toward such impulses. While the self is desireless, the body may go on in its own activities. Having renounced desire, the individual need not renounce its object.

> The man who is united with the Divine and knows the truth thinks "I do nothing at all" for in seeing, hearing, touching, smelling, tasting, walking, sleeping, breathing, speaking, emitting, grasping, opening and closing his eyes he holds that only the senses are occupied with the objects of the senses.[55]

In other words, we might say that there is a state of consciousness in which a fully functioning individual experiences himself as transcending his functions; his identity and existence are not challenged by his processes taking one course or another. His identity and his sense of beingness are anchored beyond his specific actions or forms.

The literature of mysticism describes extreme states in which we may wonder whether the cessation of craving is not an intensified form of that attribute of ego-strength and mental health to which psychological literature refers as "tolerance of frustration." What the psychologist may not regard as possible is the extrapolation of this experience to its logical extreme: equanimity in the face of death itself. We do not believe that life could be possible or meaningful if we did not cling to it in despair of dying. Yet who lives a fuller life than he who is willing to live and die for something? We do not have to look for this condition in a hero. An animal is perhaps just as adequate an example:

> But is it really necessary to survive? Is not survival, the continuation of the consistent pattern of the organism, a form of play? We must be careful of the anthropomorphism which asserts that animals hunt and eat *in order* to survive, or that a sunflower turns *in order* to keep its face to the sun. . . . When we say that an organism *likes* to go on living . . . what evidence is there for this "like" except that in fact it does go on living—until it doesn't? [56]

As the passage from the *Gita* quoted on p. 199 suggests, the quality of detachment or needlessness need not be restrictive of action. Action does not need necessity. The river does not need to be pushed.

The place of asceticism, consequently, is not among the ideals of life but among the methods for attaining such ideals —methods to be given up as the raft of which Buddhism speaks is to be abandoned upon reaching the other shore.

A Pakistani acquaintance has told me of a dervish cap that is divided into four quarters of different colors. The first stands for renunciation of this world, the second for renunciation of the other world, the third for renunciation of one's self. The fourth for renunciation of renunciation.

The function of the ascetic method is that of realizing a sameness in pleasure and in pain and attaining a freedom from the compulsion to seek the one and avoid the other—both part of a capacity to accept life in all its states. The goal of asceticism is a freedom from the need for what is not and the capacity to surrender to what is. And this capacity for acceptance of the given we can also understand as an expression of the realization that existence is enough; where we ordinarily attach ourselves to specific preferences and greedily pursue their satisfaction, when we lose awareness of a basic satisfaction of merely being.*

Unity: Resolution and Transcendence of Conflicts

Buddha said: Subhuti, all the Bodhisattva-Heroes should discipline their thoughts as follows: all living creatures of whatever class, born from eggs, from wombs, from moisture, or by transformation, whether with form or without form, whether in a state of thinking or exempt from thought-necessity, or wholly beyond all thought realms—all these are caused by Me to attain Unbounded Liberation Nirvana. Yet when vast, uncountable, immeasurable numbers of beings have thus been liberated, verily no being has been liberated. Why is this, Subhuti? It is because no Bodhisattva who is a real Bodhisattva cherishes the idea of an ego-entity, a personality, a being, or a separated individuality.[57]

—from *The Diamond Sutra*

---

* Asceticism is one means of recovering this joy of existing. Its approach is that of divesting the person of all *but* his life, until he may come to terms with it—and see it for what it is rather than for what it lacks.

Since we have learnt the Alphabet of Love,
None other text than this can we repeat:
With the heart's eyes, wide-opened now, behold
Whate'er thou see-est as but a form of His![58]
—SAADI

We have been dealing with unity in the previous sections of this chapter without bringing in the word. Unification of the usual mind-body dichotomy is achieved by following an experiential path that leads to the finding of the existence of either an intelligent body of spiritualized matter, or a God incarnate in all things and giving all things their very substance. A unity of subject and object, Man and World, is also implied; there is a state, which seems to be the limit of what we regard as human development, where this boundary is lost without loss of self-awareness. Some of this condition is part of intuitive thinking and aesthetic states, but more obviously it is an aspect of so-called cosmic consciousness. Finally, the distinction between Man and God is also reabsorbed into unity, whether this is expressed in theistic or nontheistic language. In the former case it is expressed as being one with God or part of God, and in the latter the feelings that are usually "projected" in a God image or concept are reincorporated in the world and in man. In this way, too, Man is God, the experience of Self becomes endowed with the quality of sanctity, profoundness, ineffability, and especially with that of being an end in itself.

As with the extremes of experience depicted in the previous section, these extremes of unity may seem so remote from ordinary experience that they might be thought as no more than matters of fantasy or philosophical speculation. Yet something of this nature is present in the quality of those peak-experiences that Maslow has found to be known to most people. In these, he says, "the dichotomies, polarities, and conflicts of life tend to be transcended or resolved. That is to say, there tends to be a moving toward the perception of unity and integration in the world." Furthermore, the experience of unity with the object underlies all true aesthetic experiences (as distinct from judgment of "good taste"); likewise, the experience of unity with another human being underlies the feelings of true love (as distinct from much that we call love).

But let us turn from the relatively unusual experience of feeling one with the world and other beings, with our body, with the world in ourselves, or with God, to a form or level of unity that seems to be a precondition to all others: intrapsychic unity. How can a split person feel united to anything or anybody else? Only one portion of his divided self would be able to participate in any such unification with another. How could the vision of God-in-all-things, for instance, bypass that of God in all the fragments of the psyche? Union, like so many other things, begins at home.

The coincidence of metaphysical opposites enumerated above and the integration of the psyche may be said to be aspects of a single experience, and yet one or the other aspect may predominate in the awareness of an individual describing it or trying to interpret it. Because of this, perhaps, it sometimes seems that a realization in the nature of a philosophical insight leads to psychological integration, while at other times a resolution of psychological conflicts leads to feelings of unity with other aspects of the world, beings, or reality at large— maybe in the form of peak-experiences. Just as it seems clear that these peak-experiences are more frequent in persons who are emotionally healthy, it is clear that they are healing as well. Commenting upon the aspect of unity, Maslow states:

> To have a clear perception (rather than a purely abstract and verbal philosophical acceptance) that the universe is all of a piece

and that one has his place in it—one is a part of it, one belongs in it—can be so profound and shaking an experience that it can change the person's character and his Weltanschauung forever after. In my own experience I have two subjects who, because of such an experience, were totally, immediately, and permanently cured of (in one case) chronic anxiety neurosis and (in the other case) of strong obsessional thoughts of suicide.[59]

As to the peak-experience itself, this is one in which the individual may be regarded as temporarily healed. Not only does he perceive the universe as a unified whole but, to quote Maslow again, "The person himself tends to move toward fusion, integration, and unity and away from splitting, conflicts, and oppositions." [60]

Though both aspects of unification, transpersonal and intrapersonal, have been recognized in the traditional spiritual disciplines and in psychotherapy as a whole, their respective emphases differ. The healer is mainly concerned with the resolution of internal conflicts, compartmentalizations, and inconsistencies while the mystic seeks union with the Divine Being. Psychotherapy stresses the balance of right and left; mysticism the harmony of above and below.

Expressions such as "integration of personality" (Jung), "psychosynthesis" (Assagioli), "harmonious development of man" (Gurdjieff), stem from the recognition that the ordinary state of man, and to a much greater extent the pathological, are marked by conflict, splits, dissociation, and contradiction between psychological functions or personality fragments. Indeed, it was a momentous contribution of Freud to point out that every symptom was the expression of a conflict. And yet most internal conflicts are themselves no more than the particularized manifestation of more generalized conflicts between basic urges or sub-selves. While these exist, there can hardly be a single moment or action not endowed with some conflictive quality, even though it may be subliminal and unrecognized. Freud viewed these as conflicts between superego, ego, and id —the internalized norms of civilization, the demands of reality, and the innate urges. Jung stresses the conflict between the different functions of the ego—thinking, feeling, sensing, intuiting—as well as those between the introversive and extraversive tendencies. Horney speaks of a central conflict that constitutes the ground of all others: that between the real self and the idealized self or false personality. These are all different angles of approach to the same issues. Whatever the terminology and point of view, a reconciliation and collaboration between the major aspects of psychological life are sought, whether in terms of "conciliation of opposites" (Jung), "transcendence of opposites" (psychosynthesis), Buddha's "middle path," Confucius's "golden mean," or other approaches to the wholeness of the human being.

In practice, the first step made by most psychotherapists is that of exposing the conflict; bringing into conscious light the elements in struggle which may be hidden behind a cloud of discomfort, guilt, fear, or shame. Such feelings usually stem from the clash between a condemning sub-self and the condemned feelings, urges, or thoughts, the aim or function of which is not recognized. This process of laying out the conflicts may be regarded as a step toward their resolution in itself, for it is the attention to both sides of the conflict that eventually leads to their mutual recognition, respect, and collaboration. Such listening to the parts in dispute, while very systematic in Gestalt therapy where they are enacted so that the person finds what is at stake for him in the alternatives, is also a regular occurrence in every form of insight psychotherapy and meditation approach based on attention to the spontaneous stream of consciousness. Probably the practice of systematic evaluation of one's actions, as in the Jesuits' "examination of consciousness" at the end of the day, is effective in bringing out the conflict between a person's standards and his perceived reality, and thus leads to the refinement and adjustment of both his values and feelings.

Somewhat related in function to the uncovering of conflicts, aiming toward the eventual wholeness of the person, is the development of undeveloped functions or attitudes, the reinforcement of suppressed or repressed aspects of the personality. For unity to be achieved, the pseudounity consisting in the supremacy of a part must give way to a polarity. Again, this is something that takes place naturally in any attempt at self-exploration or self-expression, from psychoanalysis to art. It is also an important aspect of risk-taking groups and role-playing, where the person may be specifically directed to the enacting of his counterstyles, thus creating some flexibility in the ordinary personality.

Once the opposing tendencies in conflict are exposed, we can conceive of two alternative approaches toward a possible unification: one, a deepening in the understanding of each, until a common ground may be discovered that allows for their collaboration; the other, the orientation of both toward a third, extrinsically given possibility. The first is a movement into the dissenting voices, a merging with the parts or a descent as we have already described it; the second entails a movement away from both parts in conflict, a detachment from them in a movement of ascent. As I mentioned earlier, there is a preponderance of the former attitude in psychotherapy, and of the latter in religion, while the third possibility, over and above internal conflicts, is generally a symbol of the Complete Man or of the Deity or a model of right action.

This idea of attaining a balance by subordinating both parts of a conflict to a higher purpose, is symbolized by a floor of black and white tiles in some masonic temples: both "good" and "evil" are of the same value in supporting the altarpiece. This notion is also literally applied in the specific form of meditation that observes the succession of mental events and dedicates each to the ultimate goal or to the image of the deity.[61] In this process, which, like ritual, entails an "as if" situation from the point of view of the subject, the individual may discover that all of him really has a function and deserves to be offered. Such harmonization of contradictions as a consequence of the subordination of conflicts to a fervent aspiration may explain both the integrative repercussion of the devotional ways and the well-being frequently resulting from any kind of deep enthusiasm. A particularly significant form of this is represented by an intense urge for self-transformation in the therapeutic process which alone permits a person to open up to both the "best" and "worst" in his inner life.

The two processes of transcendence-detachment and of enhanced merging seem to be opposed: *resolution* of conflicts seeks an intrinsic ground of unity beyond apparent opposition, a source-urge beyond the dual differentiation; while *transcendence* of conflicts finds an extrinsic alternative to which the opposed tendencies become subordinated. But is this extrinsic alternative not a symbolic prefiguration of the still unrealized intrinsic unity?

This may be seen most clearly when we consider approaches that lie between these two extremes; where a psychological silence is encouraged to favor a third possibility, which is not externally given in the form of traditional symbols or solutions. An instance of this we find in Meher Baba's statement to the effect that conflict can be solved through true valuation:

There is a world of difference between necessity and importance. Many things come to the ego as being necessary, but they are not in themselves important. Spirituality, which comes to the ego as being unnecessary, is really important for the soul. The ego thus represents a deep and fundamental principle of ignorance which is exhibited in *always preferring the unimportant to the important.*

In contrast:

If the mind is to be freed from conflict it must always make the right choice and must unfailingly prefer the truly important to the unimportant. *The choice has to be both intelligent and firm in all cases of conflict—important as well as unimportant.* It has to be intelligent, because only through the pursuit of true and permanent values is it possible to attain a poise which is not detrimental to the dynamic and creative flow of mental life. An intelligent choice, if it is stern, may temporarily overcome conflict, but it is bound in the long run to curtail the scope of life or to hamper the fulfillment of the whole personality. Moreover, the conflict will surely reappear in some other form if it has not been intelligently solved. An intelligent solution, on the other hand, requires an *insight into true values,** which have to be disentangled from false values. The problem of the conflict of desires thus turns out to be the problem of conflicting values, and *the solution of mental conflict therefore requires a deep search for the real meaning of life.* It is only through wisdom that the mind can be freed from conflict.

Having once known what the right choice is, the next step is to stick to it firmly. Although the competing tendencies in the mind may be quieted by choosing one particular course in preference to other alternatives, they still continue to act as obstacles in making the choice fully effective and operative. At times there is a danger of a decision being subverted through the intensification of those competing psychic forces. To avoid defeat the mind must stick tenaciously to the right value which it has seen. Thus *the solution of mental conflict requires not only perception of right values but also an unswerving fidelity to them.*

The intelligent and firm choice, however, has to be repeatedly

* These italics are the author's.

exercised in *all* matters—small or great—for *the ordinary "worries" of life are not in any way less important than the serious "problems" with which the mind is confronted in times of crisis.*[62]

To Meher Baba the beginning of right valuation lies in the establishment of the true ideal, and is therefore in the nature of understanding.

Right valuation in turn is the undoing of the constructions of the ego, which thrives on false valuation. *Any action which expresses the true values of life contributes towards the disintegration of the ego, which is a product of ages of ignorant action.* Life cannot be permanently imprisoned within the cage of the ego. It must at some time strive towards the Truth. In the ripeness of evolution comes the momentous discovery that *life cannot be understood and lived fully as long as it is made to move round the pivot of the ego.* Man is then driven by the logic of his own experience *to find the true centre of experience and reorganise his life in the Truth.* This entails the wearing out of the ego and its replacement by Truth-consciousness. The disintegration of the ego culminates in realising the Truth. *The false nucleus of consolidated sanskaras* must disappear if there is to be a true integration and fulfillment of life.*[63]

The replacement of the ego (more precisely, the divided ego) by truth consciousness, here mediated by the development of intuition, is also the point of the exercises involving the voluntary cessation of some psychological phenomena, as in some forms of meditation. Such emptying the mind of thoughts or feelings requires a flexibility to allow the unexpected to enter it—for this emptiness is a state of suspension of preconceptions. In contrast, in a state of conflict a given feeling, thought, or desire is standing in the way of another, and it will not *give*. The approach of relaxation at all levels—physical, emotional, intellectual—is one of developing a certain

---

* Which means impressions or conditionings.

amount of detachment that may allow for flexibility in the interplay of psychological forces.

The difference between these approaches and the use of structured movements, rituals, prayers, or *mantras* as objects of meditation is that in all these the meditation object serves as an integrative symbol: a form which, like a catalyst, may bring out or mirror the individual's deepest urges where conflicting motives converge or coincide. These symbols operate upon the feelings from the ideational or motor level. Certain feelings will be evoked by their symbolic quality which will then be synchronized with the person's ongoing physical or mental activity; the moment of congruence thus achieved will facilitate further unification. Gurdjieff, in speaking of such integration between body, feelings, and the intellectual function, compares it to a coach with its horse and driver, and points out that what is needed is a development of reins that go between driver and horse, and shafts between the horse and the coach.

The alternative strategy to unification is that of merging into each side in the conflict and knowing it by indwelling, in the act of expression or introspection. Most conflicts stem from a judgmental act of the ego by which the personal reality is divided into goodness and badness according to some set of internalized norms (which in pathological conditions take the form of a compulsive system rather than a notion of the desirable). Therefore, the process of exploration may proceed into the "should" system (Horney), "superego" (Freud), or "top dog" (Perls) or into a system containing all the rejected aspects of psychic life, the suppression of which creates an imbalance, and the conflicting presence of which is manifested half-consciously or unconsciously in symptoms. This is the domain of

Jung's "shadow," and most of what is expressed in therapeutic catharsis or abreaction.

 ' The elements of looking-into and letting-out—self-insight and self-expression—are major ingredients of most ways of growth (if not all), and they can be looked at as the building of a bridge between the conscious and the unconscious, between the feeling-instinctual and the rational. The combined process of expression-insight is at the same time one of knowledge, liberation, and self-valuation: experience tells us that there are turning points where something in our inner lives, once truly known or contacted, is found to be acceptable and possible to express. Thus, the incorporation of personality fragments into the organic unity and the bridging process leading to such unity cannot be separated from the movement in the direction of greater freedom and self-acceptance that we are discussing in the following sections.

Depth-psychotherapy achieves a balancing of personality by bringing the postponed, undeveloped, and avoided unconscious into focus and operation. The same, though, may be said of all expressive acts: art, true friendship, the spontaneous inventive storytelling of some parents to their children, encounter groups, and the radical letting-go involved in the Subud *latihan* or in psychedelic experiences. One particular technique that deserves to be underlined in this connection as being of great potential in the exploration of the unconscious is hypnotic abreaction. It also suggests a strategy of wider applicability because in the hypnotic situation a person may dare to open up to feelings, memories, or thoughts that he would not ordinarily recognize, experience, or express because *he* is not there as a witness. The process may be pictured as one in which he can allow all that he fears because *he* is not exposed to it. Everything happens behind his back, and outside his responsibility. *He* is asleep, and when he wakes up he will feel free to forget it again. Yet one of the values of the approach lies in the fact that when his delegated self remembers, feels, utters the avoided and unforgivable, he finds out that there is nothing so unbearable in it after all. The whole event may be conceived as an "as if" situation, a role being played by the assumed unconsciousness, which "tricks" itself into manifestation and provides the opportunity for new learning: as in other approaches, the person learns that there was nothing to fear but his preconceptions and fantasies. This same strategy is not restricted to hypnosis. To some extent it is part of behavior therapy, in which the patient meets the avoided under optimum conditions, and especially in psychodrama, guided reveries, or any expressive acts in a symbolic medium: in all these the person is allowing himself to express aspects of himself that would not emerge so easily if it were not for the make-believe quality of such expression. For the symbol not only embodies but substitutes: the persona can always experience it as "not really me." If this is true of much art and dream experience, it is even truer of the spectator: his cathartic experience is made possible, sometimes, by symbolic participation in what he would not risk to live. Thus art plays a role which at the same time reminds man of his deepest feelings and therefore keeps him alive, and substitutes their direct expression for vicarious experience. If symbolic expression and participation are a bridge to (or from) the unconscious, they are only part of the bridge, which calls for an extra step of explicitation of experience or desymbolization. There can be no question as to the potential of art if followed by proper meditation or reflection, and this is no doubt the natural way of the true artist.

What is said of art may also be said of dreams, a form of symbolic expression that we all share and which constitutes, perhaps, our most spontaneous activity. Dream symbolism expresses us better than concepts can, but it stands as an entity separated from us, a not-I. It is a message from our depths, but only when we understand its language and recognize it as our own expression. Psychotherapy has paid a great deal of attention to dreams, whether in terms of interpreting them (psychoanalysis), underlining their archetypal qualities (Jungian analysis), or unfolding their contents through enactment (psychodrama, Gestalt therapy). Yet aside from the therapy context, there is a sharp split between our dream life and our conscious concern for it (which seems characteristic of our culture). This is not the case in the so-called primitive cultures, and especially in those where shamanism is more alive. Among these, a pervasive interest in dreams goes hand in hand with a collaborative relationship between ego and nonego—whether body, tribesman, or nature.

A particular approach to dream life that deserves mention among the ways of growth presented in this book is their systematic handling among the Senoi, a rather isolated culture in Malaya. It is an established custom among this people that at the beginning of every day the family discusses the previous night's dreams, while each head of the family is to some extent a dream expert. Not only are the dreams told and listened to; they are evaluated, and the father gives advice to the children. A child may have dreamed that he was falling, for instance, and the father may comment, "There must have been a purpose in your fall. The spirit of the depth must have been pulling you down. What did you see under you?" And if the child just did not see anything in his nightmarish panic, he may be given the advice to look where he is going next time and discover the purpose of the fall. Eventually, the child may have a subsequent dream where he starts to fall, but remembering the advice, he stops resisting it, and falling turns to flying. When his father hears this report he may still feel that this dream is

unfinished, for the child has not found anything or met anybody, and his further directions will modify subsequent dreaming until the child learns something from the dream. A dream
is considered complete among the Senoi only when the
dreamer has found something in it that he can bring back to
the community: a new song, a dance, an invention, an idea.

I have touched on only one aspect of the Senoi's handling of
dream material, but this may suffice to point out the possibility of a cultivation of dream life and the establishment of a
link between the activities of the dreaming and the wakeful
mind. The subject is led into an attitude of taking responsibility and feeling himself to be a doer of his dreams, as he is of his
conscious actions, and he learns how to master his dreams
without detracting from their spontaneity and revelation quality. On the contrary, he learns how to live them out to the fullest, just as an artist learns to develop a theme to its fullest expression. Since dreaming is a symbolic display of a person's
feeling life, the practice of the Senoi seems a salutary cultural
means of developing unity between feeling, thinking, and
doing.

Self-acceptance vs. Self-rejection

An old man and his son worked a piece of land with only a horse
for help. One day the horse ran away. "How terrible," sympa-
thized the neighbors. "What bad luck."

"Who knows whether bad luck or good luck?" the old man replied.

A month later the horse returned from the mountains with a
group of wild horses. His son rounded them up.

"Wonderful! What good luck!" said the neighbors.

"Good luck? Bad luck? Who knows?" answered the farmer.

Days later, his son, trying to break a wild horse, broke his leg.

"What bad luck!"

"Bad luck? Good luck?"

The army came into the village to conscript all the young men for war. The young farmer was of no use to them because of his broken leg. Good? Bad?

—Chinese story

What has been the object of our investigation in the preceding sections may be also examined from the point of view of self-acceptance. We may see in self-rejection what separates man from part of his experience, deprives him of the knowledge of what or who he is, creates conflicts, and takes away from the freedom to be himself in the surrendering to his own style and calling.

The rejection in the early years of life arrests the individual's growth, and the whole therapeutic process may be seen as one of undoing the resulting self-rejection in order to bring about self-acceptance, self-appreciation, and self-love.

In religious terms, this process can be described as one in which man rediscovers his cosubstantiality with the divine nature, and comes closer to seeing the world and himself as God did on the seventh day of Genesis, when He saw that His creation was good.

Self-rejection is behind all the psychological symptoms— particularly anxiety and depression—just as self-acceptance is the basis for enjoyment of life. And beyond the usual range of our joys, the mystics would tell us, is the utter self-love of the divine being toward himself when our ego melts and realizes its unity with the essential oneness of existence.

There is a close connection between the question of nonacceptance and that of coercion, whether external or intrapsychic. Parental authority may express and convey to the child a lack of acceptance of his ways, and become internalized as self-coercion and self-hate. This lack of unity and of inner freedom is only another aspect of the fact that the person is not living "from within," unfolding his organismic potential, but according to an ideal image that he believes he is or should be. Self-rejection proceeds from a fantasy of "what I should be" and is directed to a phantom of "what I really am"—which never becomes known as it is nonexistent, covered up as it is by the self-image. For this reason, there is an indissoluble relationship between self-acceptance and true self-knowledge. Since what is rejected is only a fantasy, expectation, or biased interpretation of one's actions, direct noninterpretive contact with the experience of the self is a natural corrective. True self-knowledge stirs true self-love and, conversely, only the known can be loved.

There can be little question as to the value of acceptance, appreciation, and love in the education process, whether institutional or not, but these are not simple ideas that may be carried mechanically and impersonally into action. Acceptance and love entail a subject-to-subject relationship, in addition to freedom and a personal appreciation which cannot be faked. The link between the two terms in the injunction "love thy neighbor as thyself" calls for a personal quality in those that are in the helping roles that can only be achieved by self-transformation and not by mere instrumental knowledge. The life teacher called for in the different ways of growth is the living force that can use the tool of a particular "system" toward the aim of enhancing life. By perceiving, accepting, and actually loving the essential nature of a fellow man, he can bring it out, just as the sculptor's discrimination of a form brings it out of a stone and the attention of a gardener furthers the growth of his plants.

The place of love both in infantile development and in the developmental process of psychotherapy has been highlighted so frequently that a review of the subject would be an ambitious project. John Bowlby[64] and Rene A. Spitz[65] have made some of the most enlightening contributions to the understanding of love deprivation in the early years of life, and Carl Rogers has possibly been the most articulate theorist of "unconditional positive regard" in psychotherapy. It is not too surprising to note that, beyond the particular theoretical conceptions of individual psychotherapists, the more successful practitioners of the art seem to share a common quality of greater warmth and supportiveness when compared to the less experienced ones.

The central importance of love, support, and true appreciation (as distinct from compulsive approval) for an individual's growth may be understood in terms of his need for the development of self-support, self-appreciation, and self-love. If the transformation process is seen as one of death and rebirth (where the outer man with his manipulations of the world must give way to the true manifestation of the inner), love is the force that can permit the act of letting go and finding the unknown child in the heart; the process which may counteract acquired vulnerabilities until the moment when the individual knows himself well enough to trust his own nature.

Besides the touchstone of a genuine personal relationship, two other elements are very relevant in the ways of growth from the point of view of the issue of self-acceptance: self-knowledge and self-realization or self-expression. The connection between the process of achieving self-insight (experiential self-knowledge) and self-acceptance lies, as the Freudian notion of the unconscious typically conveys, in the fact that we ignore, deny, or repress what we reject. This constitutes a vicious circle, for not only do we restrict our awareness of ourselves in the process of rejecting our experience, but self-ignorance perpetuates self-rejection. Much of the subtle self-rejecting that pervades and impoverishes ordinary life is a residue of childish patterns that persist in the form of a play of the imagination: we are afraid of falling short of our idealized self and of letting our hidden monster come out of its dark cave in the soul. Whole moral philosophies and cultural styles are impregnated. with an assumption of man's basic evil that bespeaks such fear of a bogeyman within. The therapeutic process is one of finding out that there is nothing to fear, and learning through self-knowledge the worth of each grain of sand in creation. Furthermore, the blissful condition associated with enlightenment is the direct consequence of "seeing into one's true nature" (*kensho*). For, in religious terms, the full experience of knowing who I am is that which prompts the psalmist to utter "verily, ye are Gods!"

The importance of self-expression in the development of self-acceptance lies partly in the interpersonal situation, in the context of which this expression takes place. No amount of love or support is enough to somebody hiding behind a mask, for he will never know whether *he* or the role that he is presenting is really the recipient of attention and acceptance. "What if I appeared as I am?" he is liable to feel, "then I would not be acceptable any longer."

Risk-taking in interpersonal contacts, as stressed in encounter groups and self-disclosure in general, from ritual confession to Jourard's "transparent self" approach, provides the occasion to experience one's self as the target of either acceptance or rejection. On the other hand, self-expression even outside of the interpersonal context is a step toward self-acceptance because of its link with the act of consciousness: we are largely unconscious of what we do not express and can only feel ourselves in our actions, outer or inner. In expressing or realizing ourselves (i.e., making ourselves real) we step from the state of potentiality to that of substantial events through which we disclose ourselves to ourselves. This represents another aspect of the value of the arts in the developmental process, especially when not taken as a means to an external end but as an occasion for self-discovery.

In looking at different systems or procedures from the point of view of their bearing on the experience of self-acceptance, we must consider that self-acceptance is not different from the acceptance of our experience of moment after moment, as discussed in connection with the issues of self-experience and the experience of reality vs. fantasy. We might say that the openness to experience, the expression of self-acceptance at a given moment, is but the first degree in an attitude that can grow into *joy in experiencing:* an expression of self-love (not narcissism, which is love of ego), a love of existence as given in that moment.

This is the affective component in peak-experiences, probably independent of the "pleasurable" or "painful" nature of the stimulation on a sensory level.* A distinction between such affective component and pleasure proper is apparent in the following episode from Huxley's well-known description of a mescaline experience:

> I was seeing what Adam had seen on the morning of his creation
> —the miracle, moment by moment, of naked existence.
> "Is it agreeable?" somebody asked. . . .
> "Neither agreeable nor disagreeable," I answered. "It just *is*." [66]

From the point of view of self-acceptance we can distinguish two approaches which are characteristic of specific techniques, and which we have encountered in our previous discussions. One is permissive, expressive, unstructured, and destructuring; the other is restrictive or ascetic.

---

* Parenthetically, I might mention that acceptance of the world and self is a salient trait of peak-experiences. In the words of Maslow: "the world . . . is seen only as beautiful, good, desirable, worthwhile, etc. and is never experienced as evil or undesirable. The world is accepted."

The first insists on a temporary letting go of control, bound-aries, and judgments in order to experience our reality with fresh eyes. This will eventually result in the gradual relin-quishing of conditioned and obsolete reactions in which we turn against our organism and spontaneous functioning. The technique of free association is a good example at the verbal level and sensory awareness is one at the nonverbal level. Charlotte Selver has specifically stressed this aspect in speak-ing of Elsa Gindler and her work:

> She has made it her life's work to explore to what degree we human beings cooperate with the forces of nature, for instance: with spontaneous development of energy within a given activity, with the processes of life and regeneration as they happen through us, with the dynamics of rest and activity, how we respond to gravity, and so on. She has found out that in the process of this ex-ploration one can discover through sensing, how hindering tend-encies come about. As the individual becomes more sensitized and learns to befriend himself with the potentials he gradually uncov-ers, the way slowly opens to a fuller experiencing and deeper re-lating to himself and all activities of daily living.[67]

Just as the key word of sensory awareness (and expressive techniques in general) is *allowing*, that of the other group of procedures is *accepting*. These are words that relate to the two aspects of freedom that we examined in an earlier passage. *Al-lowing* suggests the unfolding of a natural process and refers to a reliance upon our spontaneity. *Accepting* applies to the toler-ance of what potentially opposes our preferences. What we tend to reject, in turn, is that which gives rise to inner states that we are not accepting or to which we are not open. Thus the two principles meet and constitute two aspects of self-ac-ceptance: the acceptance of impulse, and the acceptance of impulse-frustration. It might be further argued that acceptance of frustration itself depends upon an acceptance of the impulse that is being subject to frustration. As an illustration of this, sexual frustration in a person who accepts his sexuality is experienced as unfulfilled desire that is not painful and as a sensation of intense vitality. For a person who harbors guilt feelings in connection with sexual desire or interprets lack of fulfillment as rejection, this lack may be properly called frustration, and leads to depression and an unpleasantness calling for compulsive satisfaction and a narcotizing restriction in awareness.

There is obviously a wide range of differences in the ability to bear physical or moral pain with a positive attitude, and the gamut may reach as far as wholehearted acceptance of the greatest of "evils"—death itself. The "craft of dying" is well documented in Christian, Tibetan, and Japanese sources, and represents the extreme situation calling for the ultimate manifestation of that "sameness in pleasure and pain" of which the *Bhagavad-Gītā* speaks. From the angle of acceptance of or openness to experience, the greater challenges are those of remaining open to the more unpleasant sides of existence. It is potential unpleasantness that sets into action the filtering mechanism in our mind, restricting our awareness in proportion to our fear. If we conceive that an attitude of openness in spite of pain may be trained by exposure to conscious suffering and the commonly avoided aspects of our lives, we may understand the functional aspect of practices that range all the way from the painful initiation ordeals of primitive peoples, to asceticism and desensitization in behavior therapy. Because of the roughness of existence we are usually only half-present in our world, and all these practices challenge us not to withdraw from ourselves in the unpleasantness of fatigue, humiliation, fear, or pain. These practices aim at increasing our ability to stay in touch with our own selves through the diverse conditions of life, in a commitment that echoes that of the bride and groom who commit themselves to stay together "in sickness and in health, for better or for worse, for richer or for poorer."

Awakening

Compared with what we ought to be, we are only half awake. Our fires are damped, our drafts are checked. We are making use of only a small part of our possible mental and physical resources.[68]

—WILLIAM JAMES

Mindfulness leads to the deathless path.

—BUDDHA

Another way of looking at the experience we are discussing is in terms of consciousness. Becoming conscious of the unconscious is the aim of depth psychotherapy; consciousness expansion is almost a synonym for the psychedelic venture, heightened states of consciousness are sought in meditation, and awareness is cultivated in such contemporary approaches as sensory awareness, Gestalt therapy, and sensitivity training.

The mystical and esoteric traditions are permeated with the notion of levels of consciousness ranging from sleep to full awakening, our ordinary state being regarded as not far removed from that of dreaming. This is not difficult to accept if we consider not only the limits of our consciousness but the extent to which our action is guided by fantasies and our mind engaged in daydreaming.*

Enlightenment, therefore, is full awakening, the idea of

---

* In Vedanta the states of dream and dreamless sleep are regarded as higher than that of wakefulness which seems to contradict the goal of increased consciousness. This is only a semantic contradiction, though, for in practical terms the aim is to unite consciousness with the dream state and even with that of dreamless sleep; i.e., to become conscious of the unconscious; or, in other words, to become conscious of a domain of experience transcending the perceptive functions of wakefulness and even the feeling-imaginative activity of dreams.

"light" (which is at the root of the word *God* in many languages) being the most natural metaphor for the "light of consciousness." The Buddha essentially means the "awakened one." The notion that humanity is asleep is a central one in Sufism, and is found in derivations of it like the Gurdjieff school.

In Christianity this idea is not as evident or widely recognized, but this is only a matter of stress. The Gospels abound in passages where "being asleep" is to be taken metaphorically, and Saint Thomas Aquinas defines original sin as a "languor" of the soul that disrupts the harmony of original justice. Dante, too, describes his condition at the beginning of his spiritual quest as one of being lost in a dark wood as a consequence of having fallen asleep.

In dealing with growth-healing-enlightenment as a process of awakening with a more developed consciousness as its goal, we must realize that we are not speaking of another ingredient in such a process and state, but only of a shifting of our point of view to describe the same single inner event that has been our theme throughout this chapter. What we examined as a search for true identity (the experience of being one's self rather than living up to and identifying with an image) requires *contact* with self, a contact which is consciousness. The relinquishing of a false identity in the process of contacting the reality of experience, is part of the shift from dreamlike functioning of the mind to awareness proper. The apparent opposites of empathetic identification and detachment are part of the phenomenology of wakefulness as well: "we" step so little into the shoes of our "dream self" or other dream characters that we forget them very easily. And yet, while dreaming we are submerged in them to the point of forgetting our independent existence as dreamers. In artistic perception, which illustrates exalted awareness, empathy, and differentiation, the experience of "I am that" and the one of "I am not that" (an experience described in psychology of art as "aesthetic distance") go hand in hand. The relationship between the experience of freedom and that of consciousness is obvious enough since freedom means voluntary action, while unconscious action is involuntary and automatic. Consciousness reveals "the truth that sets me free." We have already commented upon the connection between consciousness and self-acceptance in terms of how we can only love what we know, knowing being an act of consciousness.

The connection between consciousness and unity derives from the fact that it is the split between conscious and unconscious aspects of personality that underlie most of our intraphysic conflicts. Just as it may not be possible to achieve unity of purpose or action in a group of persons unless their different views are voiced and their points of agreement discovered, it is not possible to attain unity among our inner "I's" unless they make themselves evident. When we are fully conscious of their wants we may be surprised to discover that they are all much the same. Unity, therefore, is not so much something that may be *achieved* as something that is *realized*—in an act of consciousness.

If the process of growth-enlightenment-healing is one of developing consciousness, we should be able to look at all practical systems or techniques as ways to this end. I think that we can do this in spite of their not always being expressed explicitly in these terms. The ancient disciplines of meditation are overtly aimed at the cultivation of consciousness, while the contemporary systems, grouped as insight therapies, stress in a different way the act of becoming conscious of psychic processes. In contrast to the psychoanalytic and related schools there has been a growing interest in the noninterpretive aspects of insight psychotherapy (typically in Gestalt therapy) and more generally a realization of the importance of sensing and feeling rather than understanding reality intellectually. This may be seen, for instance, in the practice of sensory awareness (where the physical aspects of experience are stressed) and in sensitivity training (where the stress is on the feelings and in the interpersonal situation). This trend represents a movement in the direction of the Eastern approach, which regards sensing-feeling as closer to reality and our interpretation of sensing-feeling as removed from and a substitute for real knowledge. Like Gestalt therapy, the Eastern disciplines place great weight on the act of simple awareness and attention to the immediacy of experience.

The seventh factor of Buddha's Noble Eightfold Path leading to the Extinction of Suffering is usually translated as "right mindfulness." In accordance with the canon, monks are repeatedly instructed by Buddha to be continuously mindful of their bodies, feelings, states of mind, objects of consciousness:

> In going to a place and in coming from it, in looking at a thing and in looking away from it, in bending and in stretching, one should act with clear awareness. . . . In eating, drinking, chewing, and tasting, in the expulsion of the faeces and the urine, in walking, standing, sitting, sleeping, and waking, in speaking and in keeping silent, one should act with clear awareness.[69]

These disciplines, which are forms of external meditation, are intended to be practiced throughout a lifetime while some of the modern approaches aim at shorter periods of time under the direction of a teacher.

Because consciousness is consciousness of something revealed in enlightenment, it is inseparable from wisdom, understood as knowledge that transcends the intellect. The knower and the unknown, consciousness and being may be viewed either from the point of view of what they contribute to the development of consciousness and of the knower (typically meditation), or what they do in terms of pointing at the unknown. In the range of ordinary psychological experience, the object of knowledge is the sum of a person's psychological events, and the act of pointing at them may range from Rogerian "reflecting" to psychoanalytic interpretations. In the mystic's terms, though, as in the Socratic "know thyself," the self to be known is not the outward appearance of psychological events, but an essence which can only be understood as Self, God, Tao, or Void. In place of personal interpretations, we find here the interpretation of the ultimate reality (of which the person is only an individual embodiment), the symbols of the hidden secret which pervade religious thought and art. These symbols cannot substitute an understanding or realization of the truth, which is beyond intellectual comprehension, but they point at it "like fingers pointing at the moon" (as Zen puts it), and as a system they mark the path of gnani yoga, the way of knowledge. Thus, in the field of religious experience, just as in everyday experience, we find methods that stress either direct experiencing or intellectual anticipating and interpreting of experience. In psychotherapy, this is the difference between psychoanalysis and the more recent noninterpretive approaches like Gestalt therapy. In the history of religion we witness the constant clash between mystics and theologians.

Aside from the approaches aimed at the development of awareness and those that facilitate insight via intellectual development or symbolic sensitization, any system that exposes the individual to unusual experiences, that requires going beyond the ordinary limits, and invites self-expression has the outcome of showing the person "this is yourself." The more automatic or conditioned a person's ordinary existence is, the more important new situations are to engage his nonprogramed behavior and offer him a reflection of what his individuality is like, and this may be the basis of the spontaneous craving for normal experiences in some people who have been submerged in a routinary life. Since the logical opposites of routine, conventional mechanicalness, and conformity are the meaningful originality of individual expression and choice called for in the creative process, we find again another reason why the arts can be a way; not only because they provide for acts of self-realization, but since a creative act can only stem from the self, it offers the self a mirror for self-awareness.

Behavior therapy is a particular approach that deserves closer consideration from the point of view of its bearing on the field of consciousness. This is of special interest here because subjective events such as consciousness or insight are not included in its theoretical premises. Furthermore, some behavioristic psychologists have claimed that in all the change that possibly takes place as a result of exposure to other therapies, insight is superfluous, its effectiveness being due to the positive and negative reinforcement that the patient's behavior is subjected to on the part of the therapist. In spite of the interesting accounts of psychoanalysis and client-centered psychotherapies in behavioristic terms, there does not seem to be in current literature any account of the events in behavior therapy in humanistic terms. Such an account could contribute to a more unified understanding of the change process, showing the *consciousness* aspect of events which has been described at the physical end of man's psychophysical unity. This may not apply to the use of conditioned vomiting in the treatment of alcoholism, because here the result is merely the building in of a new conditioned inhibition, but may apply to deconditioning techniques (including reciprocal inhibition) where the process involved justifies classing the procedure with the ways of growth that are the theme of this writing. In such techniques conditioning principles are used to decondition rather than to create new conditioning, and it may therefore be contended that this is the part of the process which accounts for the results, even when the implanting of new, "more adequate" conditioning is being sought and held responsible for improvement. We have dealt with this as openness to experience, relevant to the issues of identity, contact with reality, and self-acceptance, but the extinction of conditioning is also a question of freedom. Under the aspect of awareness or consciousness, desensitization is above all else a desensitization to our automatic rejection of contact with certain objects, situations, or persons. A phobic reaction, thus, is not truly one of fear in the midst of experiencing something, but of fear at the expectation triggered by the sign of superficial recognition of the object. What is feared is not the object proper, but a phantom—an implicit assumption about a fantasy of the object, or a catastrophic anticipation of the experience of facing it. To the extent that the desensitization process consists of training and experiencing contact rather than avoiding it, it is a training in both acceptance and consciousness. The rejection of an object, situation, or thought is only a means of rejecting the consciousness thereof, and the learning process leading to the change is probably not in the nature of a new label calling the experience "good" rather than "bad," but a learning that there is nothing to fear, and that consciousness takes place in a domain that is distinct from that where we apply such qualifications.

Summing up the essentials of this chapter, we may end by reasserting that the end-state sought by the various traditions, schools, or systems under discussion is one that is characterized by *the experience* of openness to the reality of every moment, freedom from mechanical ties to the past, and surrender to the laws of man's being, one of living in the body and yet in control of the body, in the world and yet in control of circumstances by means of the power of both awareness and independence. It is also an experience of self-acceptance, where "self" does not stand for a preconceived notion or image but is the experiential self-reality moment after moment. Above all, it is an *experience of experiencing*. For this is what consciousness means, what openness means, what surrendering leads into, what remains after the veils of conditioned perception are raised, and what the aim of acceptance is. And since experiencing is a personal matter it cannot be properly described, defined, or conveyed in words. It is a secret of secrets that remains unexplained, however much it may be talked about; a subtle quality in the great man, conveyed more through his presence than by his words, for, as Lao Tzu says: "The way that can be named is not the real way."

REFERENCE NOTES

CHAPTER I: AN INTRODUCTION TO THE QUEST FOR GROWTH

1. Jiddu Krishnamurti, *Freedom from the Known*, ed. Mary Luytens (New York: Harper & Row, 1969).
2. Abraham H. Maslow, *Toward a Psychology of Being* (Princeton, N.J.: Van Nostrand, 1962).
3. *Ibid.*
4. Sam Keen, *Apology for Wonder* (New York: Harper & Row, 1969).
5. Gershom G. Scholem, ed., *Major Trends in Jewish Mysticism* (New York: Schocken Books, 1955).
6. René Guénon, *Man and His Becoming According to the Vedanta*, tr. Richard C. Nicholson (London: Luzac & Co., 1945).
7. Herbert Otto and John Mann, eds., *Ways of Growth: Approaches to Expanding Awareness* (New York: Grossman Publishers, 1969).
8. Fred Fiedler, "The Concept of an Ideal Therapeutic Relationship," *Journal of Consulting Psychology* 14 (1950): 239–45; *idem,* "A Comparison of Therapeutic Relationships in Psychoanalytic, Nondirective and Adlerian Therapy," *ibid.:* 436–45.
9. Retold and commented upon by Idries Shah in *The Sufis* (Garden City, N.Y.: Doubleday & Co., 1964).

CHAPTER II: THE GOALS OF HUMAN TRANSFORMATION

1. Idries Shah, *The Exploits of the Incomparable Mulla Nasrudin* (New York: Simon & Schuster, 1966).
2. Swami Prabhavananda and Christopher Isherwood, trs., *The Song of God, Bhagavad-Gita* (London: Phoenix, 1953).
3. A. S. Neill, *Summerhill: A Radical Approach to Child Rearing* (New York: Hart, 1963).
4. Maria Montessori, *The Absorbent Mind* (Madras: Adyar, 1949).

5. Johann H. Pestalozzi, "Address on Birthday, 1818." Quoted in the *Encyclopedia of Religion and Ethics*, ed. James Hastings, s.v. "education" (New York: Charles Scribner's Sons, 1908–27).

6. Aldous Huxley, *The Perennial Philosophy* (London: Chatto & Windus, 1950).

7. Dante, *The Divine Comedy, Purgatorio* (trans. John Ciardi), canto XXXIII, 142–46. (New York: Appleton-Century-Crofts, 1971).

8. Erich Fromm, *The Art of Loving: An Enquiry into the Nature of Love* (New York: Harper and Brothers, 1956).

9. In Thomas Merton, *Raids on the Unspeakable* (New York: New Directions, 1964).

10. Ignacio Matte Blanco, "El Concepto de Enfermedad Mental," in *El Concepto de Enfermedad* (Santiago de Chile: Ediciones de la Universidad de Chile, 1963).

11. Paul Reps, ed., *Zen Flesh, Zen Bones: A Collection of Zen and Pre-Zen Writings* (New York: Doubleday & Co., 1961).

12. See, for instance, Frithjof Schuon's *The Transcendent Unity of Religions* (London: Faber and Faber, 1953).

13. Guénon, *op.cit.*

14. Louis Pauwels and Jacques Bergier, *The Dawn of Magic* (London: Anthony Gibbs & Phillips, 1963). Published in paperback edition under the title *The Morning of the Magicians* (New York: Avon Books, 1968).

15. Rafael Lefort, *The Teachers of Gurdjieff* (London: Gollancz, 1966).

16. Roy W. Davidson, *Documents on Contemporary Dervish Communities* (London: Hoopoe, 1966).

17. Idries Shah, *Tales of the Dervishes: Teaching-Stories of the Sufi Masters over the Past Thousand Years* (London: Jonathan Cape, 1967).

18. Solomon Schechter, *Aspects of Rabbinic Theology: Major Concepts of the Talmud* (New York: Schocken Books, 1961).

19. Alan Watts, *Psychotherapy East and West* (New York: Pantheon Books, 1961).

20. Bedard Boss, *A Psychiatrist Discovers India* (Chester Springs, Pa.: Dufour, 1965).

21. Erich Fromm, Daisetz T. Suzuki, and R. de Martino, *Zen Buddhism and Psychoanalysis* (New York: Grove Press, 1963).

22. H. Jacobs, *Western Psychotherapy and Hindu Sadhana: A Contribution to Comparative Studies in Psychology and Metaphysics* (London: Allen and Unwin, 1961).

23. Carl G. Jung, Psychological Commentary to *The Tibetan Book of the Dead*, by W. Y. Evans-Wentz, ed. (New York: Oxford University Press, 1957).

24. Heinrich Zimmer, "On the Significance of the Indian Tantric Yoga," *Papers from the Eranos Yearbooks: Spiritual Disciplines*, Bollingen Series XXX, No. 4 (New York: Pantheon Books, 1960).

25. Victor D. Sauna, "Religion, Mental Health and Personality: A Review of Empirical Studies," *American Journal of Psychiatry* 125 (1969): 1203–1213.

CHAPTER III: TRADITIONAL WAYS
AND CONTEMPORARY ECHOES

1. Idries Shah, *The Exploits of the Incomparable Mulla Nasrudin.*
2. Haridas Chaudhuri, *Integral Yoga: The Concept of Harmonious and Creative Living* (London: Allen and Unwin, 1965).
3. Frederic Spiegelberg, *Spiritual Practices of India* (San Francisco: Greenwood Press, 1951).
4. Trevor P. Legget, *The Tiger's Cave* (London: Rider & Co., 1967).
5. Schechter, *op. cit.*
6. *Ibid.*
7. Chaudhuri, *op. cit.*
8. Joseph Wolpe and A. Lazarus, *Behavior Therapy Techniques* (New York: Pergamon Press, 1966).
9. A. Platonov, *The Word as a Physiological and Therapeutic Factor in the Theory and Practice of Psychotherapy According to Pavlov* (Moscow: Foreign Language Publishing House, 1959).
10. J. Bennett, *Concerning Subud* (London: Hodder & Stoughton, 1960).
11. Gusty L. Herrigel, *Zen in the Art of Flower Arrangement* (London: Routledge and Kegan Paul, 1958).
12. Eugen Herrigel, *Zen in the Art of Archery* (New York: Pantheon Books, 1953).
13. Robert Frager, "The Psychology of the Samurai," *Psychology Today* (January 1969): 48.
14. *Ibid.*
15. Alan Watts, *Beyond Theology: The Art of Godmanship* (New York: World Publishing, 1967).
16. Bernard Gunther, *Getting in Touch with Massage,* Esalen Monographs (Big Sur, Calif.: 1967).
17. Cheng Man-Ching and Robert W. Smith, *Tai Chi Chuan—The Supreme Ultimate Exercise for Health, Sport and Self-Defense* (Rutland, Vt.: Charles E. Tuttle, 1967).
18. Robert S. De Ropp, *The Master Game: Pathways to Higher Consciousness beyond the Drug Experience* (New York: Delacorte Press, 1967).
19. Herbert Fingarette, *The Self in Transformation* (New York: Basic Books, 1963).
20. Frank C. Happold, *Mysticism* (London: Penguin Books, 1963).
21. Evelyn Underhill, ed., *The Cloud of Unknowing* (London: Watkins, 1946).
22. Chaudhuri, *op. cit.*
23. Charles Williams, *The Figure of Beatrice: A Study in Dante* (London: Faber and Faber, 1958). See also Mary M. Shideler, *The Theology of Romantic Love: A Study in the Writings of Williams* (New York: Harper & Row, 1962).
24. See Abraham H. Maslow, *Religions, Values, and Peak-Experiences* (Columbus: Ohio State University Press, 1964).
25. See William C. Schutz, *Joy: Expanding Human Awareness* (New York: Grove Press, 1967).

26. Claudio Naranjo and Robert E. Ornstein, *On the Psychology of Meditation* (New York: The Viking Press, 1971).

27. In Joen Fagan and Irma Lee Shepherd, eds., *Gestalt Therapy Now* (Palo Alto, Calif.: Science and Behavior Books, 1970).

28. Aldous Huxley, "The Education of an Amphibian," in *Tomorrow and Tomorrow and Tomorrow and Other Essays* (New York: Harper and Brothers, 1952).

29. In Reginald H. Blyth, *Zen and Zen Classics*, Vol. I (Tokyo: Hokuseido Press, 1960).

30. In Happold, *op. cit.*

31. *Ibid.*

32. James Jeans, *Physics and Philosophy* (New York: Cambridge University Press, 1942).

33. Edward Carpenter, *The Drama of Love and Death* (London: Allen and Unwin, 1912).

34. W. Y. Evans-Wentz, ed., *Tibetan Yoga and Secret Doctrines* (New York: Oxford University Press, 1960).

35. Daisetz T. Suzuki, *The Training of the Buddhist Monk* (Kyoto: Eastern Buddhist Society, 1934).

36. Alexander Lowen, *The Betrayal of the Body* (New York: Macmillan, 1966).

37. Fagan and Shepherd, *op. cit.*

38. L. B. Fierman, ed., *Effective Psychotherapy—The Contribution of Helmuth Kaiser* (New York: Free Press, 1965).

39. Shah, *Tales of the Dervishes.*

40. Suzuki, *op. cit.*

41. Phiroz Mehta, "Mindfulness and the Fourth Precept," *The Middle Way*, Vol. 41, No. 2, London (August 1966): 50–55.

42. Johannes Schultz and Wolfgang Luthe, *Autogenic Training: A Psychophysiologic Approach in Psychotherapy* (New York and London: Grune and Stratton, 1959).

43. Roberto Assagioli, *Psychosynthesis: A Manual of Principles and Techniques* (New York: Hobbs, Dorman, 1965).

44. Minor White, "Extended Perception through Photograph and Suggestion," in Otto and Mann, eds., *op. cit.*

45. Claudio Naranjo, *The Attitude and Practice of Gestalt Therapy* (to be published by Science and Behavior Books).

46. Robert C. Owen, *Folklore of the Mesquakie Indians* (1904).

47. David Cranz, *History of Greenland* (London: Longman, 1820).

48. Gustav F. Klemm, *Allgemeine Kulturgeschichte der Menschheit* (Leipzig: 1843–52) 3:85.

49. Karl F. von Martius, *Rechtszustände unter den Ur-Brasilianern* (Munich: 1832).

50. Martin Dobrizhoffer, *An Account of the Abipones, an Equestrian People of Paraguay* (London: J. Murray, 1822).

51. Henry Callaway, *The Religious System of the Amazulu* (London: Trubner & Co., 1884).

52. John Lilly, "Mental Effects of Reduction of Ordinary Levels of Physical Stimuli on Intact Healthy Persons," *Psychiatric Research Reports,* No. 5 (Washington, D.C.: American Psychiatric Association, 1956).

53. F. Matthias Alexander, *The Use of the Self* (Manchester: Re-Educational Publications, 1957).

54. Ladislas J. Meduna, *Carbon Dioxide Therapy* (Springfield, Ill.: Charles C. Thomas, 1950).

55. Bo Homstedt, *Ethnopharmacological Search for Psychoactive Drugs* (Washington, D.C.: U.S. Department of Health, Education and Welfare, 1968).

56. Patanjali, *The Yoga Sutras,* tr. Charles Johnston (London: Watkins, 1949).

57. Carlos Castaneda, *The Teachings of Don Juan: A Yaqui Way of Knowledge* (Berkeley, Calif.: University of California Press, 1969) and *A Separate Reality: Further Conversations with Don Juan* (New York: Simon and Schuster, 1971).

58. Reported in Castaneda, *The Teachings of Don Juan.*

59. Aldous Huxley, *Island* (New York: Harper & Row, 1962).

60. William H. Sheldon, *The Varieties of Temperament: A Psychology of Constitutional Differences* (New York: Hafner, 1969).

61. P. W. Martin, *Experiment in Depth: A Study of the Work of Jung, Eliot and Toynbee* (London: Routledge and Kegan Paul, 1955).

62. Meher Baba, *The Everything and the Nothing* (Sydney: Meher House, 1963).

63. David Bakan, *Sigmund Freud and the Jewish Mystical Tradition* (Princeton, N.J.: Van Nostrand Reinhold, 1958).

64. Anagarika B. Govinda, *The Way of the White Clouds: A Buddhist Pilgrim in Tibet* (London: Hutchinson & Co., 1966).

CHAPTER IV: THE ONENESS OF EXPERIENCE IN THE WAYS OF GROWTH

1. Karen Horney, *Neurosis and Human Growth: The Struggle toward Self-Realization* (New York: W. W. Norton & Company, 1950).

2. Carl G. Jung, "Principles of Practical Psychotherapy," in *The Practice of Psychotherapy,* Vol. 16 of *Collected Works* (New York: Pantheon Books, 1951).

3. Maxwell Maltz, *Psychocybernetics* (New York: Prentice-Hall, 1960).

4. Ronald D. Laing, *The Politics of Experience* (New York: Pantheon Books, 1966).

5. In Bhagavan Das, *The Essential Unity of All Religions* (Wheaton, Ill.: The Theosophical Publishing House, 1966).

6. *Ibid.*

7. Alan Watts, *The Book: On the Taboo against Knowing Who You Are* (New York: Collier, 1967).

8. Jung, Psychological Commentary to *The Tibetan Book of the Dead.*

9. Stanislaus Grof, *LSD: A Report on Czechoslovakian Research* (Big Sur, Calif.: Big Sur Recordings, 1968). *See also* Harold Abramson, ed., *International*

Conference on the Use of LSD in Psychotherapy and Alcoholism (Indianapolis: Bobbs-Merrill, 1966).

10. In Karlfried von Durkheim, *The Japanese Cult of Tranquility* (London: Rider & Co., 1960).

11. Alan Watts, *The Supreme Identity: An Essay on Oriental Metaphysics and the Christian Religion* (London: Faber and Faber, 1950).

12. Shrinyu Suzuki Roshi, Lecture recorded during a Sesshin, in *Wind Bell*, 5, No. 3 (1966).

13. Christmas Humphreys, ed., *The Sutra of Wei Lang (or Hui Neng)* tr. Wong Mou-Lam (London: Luzac & Co., 1944).

14. Eugen Herrigel, *op. cit.*

15. Quoted in Alexandra David-Neel, *The Secret Oral Teachings in Tibetan Buddhist Sects* (Calcutta: Maha Bodhi Society of India, n.d.).

16. Solomon Schechter, *op. cit.*

17. Kahlil Gibran, *The Madman* (New York: Knopf, 1918).

18. T. W. Adorno *et al.*, *The Authoritarian Personality* (New York: Norton, 1950).

19. Eric Hoffer, *The True Believer* (New York: Harper & Row, 1951).

20. Evelyn Underhill, *Practical Mysticism* (New York: Dutton & Co., 1915).

21. Ernst Kris, "Ego Development and the Comic," *International Journal of Psychoanalysis* (1938).

22. Frank Barron, *Creativity and Personal Freedom* (Princeton, N.J.: Van Nostrand Reinhold, 1968).

23. Ronald Taft, "Peak Experiences and Ego Permissiveness: An Exploratory Factor Study of their Dimensions in Normal Persons," *Acta Psychologica* 29, Amsterdam (February 1969): 35–64.

24. K. Dabrowski, "Positive Disintegration," tape in the Series *The Value of Psychotic Experience* (Big Sur, Calif.: Esalen Recordings, 1968).

25. Laing, *op. cit.*

26. Julian Silverman, "Shamans and Acute Schizophrenia," *American Anthropologist*, Vol. 69, No. 1 (February 1967): 21–31.

27. Dante, *The Divine Comedy, Paradiso* (trans. Barbara Reynolds), canto XXXIII, 52–63.

28. J. W. N. Sullivan, *Beethoven* (London: Penguin Books, 1949).

29. Anton Ehrenzweig, *The Psycho-Analysis of Artistic Vision and Hearing* (New York: Braziller, 1965).

30. This interesting method is described by Hoyt Sherman in his book *Drawing by Seeing—A New Development in the Teaching of Visual Art through the Training of Perception* (New York: Hinds, Hurden and Eldredge, 1947).

31. Samuel Renshaw, "The Visual Perception and Reproduction of Forms by Tachistoscopic Methods," *Journal of Psychology*, Vol. 20 (1945): 217–32.

32. Aldous Huxley, *The Doors of Perception* (New York: Harper & Row, 1954).

33. Ajit Mookerjee, *Tantra Art: Its Philosophy and Physics* (New Delhi: Ravi Kumar, 1966).

34. Ronald D. Laing, "Sanity, Madness, Blow-Out Center," tape in the Series *The Value of Psychotic Experience* (Big Sur, Calif.: Esalen Recordings, 1968).
35. Robert Desoille, *The Directed Daydream*, trans. Frank Haronian, *P.R.F.*, Issue No. 18 (New York: Psychosynthesis Research Foundation, 1966).
36. Charlotte Selver, "Sensory Awareness and Total Functioning," *General Semantics Bulletin*, Nos. 20 and 21 (1957); and Charlotte Selver and Charles Brooks, "Report on Work in Sensory Awareness and Total Functioning," in Herbert A. Otto, *Explorations in Human Potentialities* (Springfield, Ill.: Charles C. Thomas, 1966).
37. Assagioli, *op. cit.*
38. Patanjali, *op. cit.*
39. Humphreys, ed., *The Sutra of Wei Lang.*
40. Wing-Tsit Chang, tr., *The Way of Lao Tzu* (Indianapolis: Bobbs-Merrill, 1963).
41. In Reps, *op. cit.*
42. Nyaponika Thera, *Satipatthana: The Heart of Buddhist Meditation* (London: Rider & Co., 1962).
43. P. D. Ouspenski, *In Search of the Miraculous: Fragments of an Unknown Teaching* (New York: Harcourt, Brace & World, 1949).
44. De Ropp, *op. cit.*
45. Ouspenski, *op. cit.*
46. Rune Johansson, *The Psychology of Nirvana: A Comparative Study of the Natural Goal of Buddhism and the Aims of Modern Western Psychology* (London: Allen and Unwin, 1969).
47. Carl Rogers and Barry Stevens, *Person to Person: The Problem of Being Human* (Lafayette, Calif.: Real People Press, 1967).
48. Watts, *Psychotherapy East and West.*
49. Erich Fromm, *Escape from Freedom* (New York: Rinehart, 1941).
50. Rogers and Stevens, *op. cit.*
51. Spiegelberg, *op. cit.*
52. Thomas Merton, "The Spiritual Father in the Desert Tradition," *The Burke Memorial Society Newsletter-Review*, Vol. 3, No. 1 (1968).
53. Shah, *Tales of the Dervishes.*
54. André Festugière, *Personal Religion among the Greeks* (Berkeley, Calif.: University of California Press, 1954).
55. Prabhavananda and Isherwood, trs., *op. cit.*
56. Watts, *Psychotherapy East and West.*
57. Arnold F. Price, tr., *The Jewel of Transcendental Wisdom* (*Chin Kang Ching*) (London: The Buddhist Society, 1947).
58. In Bhagavan Das, *op. cit.*
59. Maslow, *Religions, Values, and Peak-Experiences.*
60. *Ibid.*
61. See Chaudhuri, *op. cit.*
62. Meher Baba, *Discourses*, Vol. II (San Francisco: Sufism Reoriented, 1967).

63. *Ibid.*
64. John Bowlby, *Child Care and the Growth of Love* (London: Pelican, 1965).
65. Rene A. Spitz, "Hospitalism. An Inquiry into the Genesis of Psychiatric Conditions in Early Childhood," *The Psychoanalytic Study of the Child* (1945): 53–74.
66. Huxley, *The Doors of Perception.*
67. Selver, "Sensory Awareness and Total Functioning."
68. William James, "The Energies of Men," in John K. Roth, ed., *The Moral Equivalent of War and Other Essays* (New York: Harper & Row, 1971).
69. Spiegelberg, *op. cit.*

INDEX